ATLANTIC SALMON
A Fly Fishing Primer

by PAUL C. MARRINER

Winchester Press
An Imprint of New Win Publishing, Inc.

Library of Congress Cataloging-in-Publication Data

Marriner, Paul C.
    Atlantic salmon : a fly fishing primer / Paul C. Marriner.
        p.   cm.
    Includes bibliographical references (p.   ) and index.
    ISBN 0-8329-0473-2 (hardcover) : $24.95
    1. Atlantic salmon fishing. 2. Fly fishing. 3. Atlantic salmon.
I. Title.
SH685.M28 1992
799.1'755—dc20   92-31271
                                                  CIP

Dedication

To Jim and Marie, who generously offered me many opportunities, and Nancy, who abided my taking them.

Acknowledgments

Every writer owes a debt to many, and the fear of forgetting someone is ever present. Despite that, I press on while issuing apologies when needed.

I would like to thank Cliff Brown, who taught me how to fish for salmon; Jim Marriner, Jerry Williamson, Len Rich, Jane Cleaves and Bill Taylor of the Atlantic Salmon Federation, Liz Wylie, Brian Rodehouse, Alex Mills, John Huff, Donald Thom, Doug Haney, Jack Swedberg, and the New Brunswick Department of Economic Development and Tourism for permission to use their photographs; Milton MacKay for flies and photographs; Heather Bale for the illustrations. Bill Ensor for reading the manuscript, making several of my excursions possible, and for the use of his photographs; Bethe Andreasen for reading the manuscript; Bill Hooper of the Fish and Wildlife Branch of the New Brunswick government, who has supplied me with statistics and many valuable insights; Bill Bryson for comments on Nova Scotia rivers; Mike and Denise Maxwell for photographs and assistance in describing spey casts; Jerry Doak for sample flies and historical information on the flies of the Miramichi; Bill McClure (The Sportsman's Cabinet) and John Moldenhauer (Rising Trout) for helping me locate books on Atlantic salmon fishing over the years; various officials in the Federal Department of Fisheries and Oceans, particularly Gary Stevens in Halifax, for providing statistical data; Denis Dorion of the Ministère du Loisir, de la Chasse et de la Pêche, for the statistical information on Quebec rivers; the publishers of *Fly Fisherman* and *Flyfishing* for permission to reprint portions of articles which have previously appeared in their pages; and finally, all the salmon fishers I have met beside the rivers who have been generous with courtesy, fellowship, and information.

Contents

INTRODUCTION

Salmon fishing is often considered a pastime of the wealthy. Sadly, this reputation is partly deserved. Certainly, with a few notable exceptions, first-class fishing for the largest specimens is beyond the means of most fly-fishers. There are, however, plenty of opportunities for the rest of us.

Virtually all my salmon have been caught in public waters. For that reason, and because I'm assuming that that is where you are most likely to fish, I concentrate on the situations where you are sharing the pools with others. As Len Wright put it in the book *Fly-Fishing Heresies* (1975), ''If someone has been kind enough to leave you several miles of big-fish river complete with lodge or a vault full of blue-chip securities to buy your way in, read no further. You should catch plenty of big salmon without any advice from the cheap seats.''

Not long ago I was introducing a relatively experienced fly-fisher to salmon fishing, and his observation, though he was enjoying himself, was that salmon fishing seemed to depend heavily on luck, requiring little in the way of additional skills. I thought this judgment was premature, since it was based on only a couple of days on the river, but I understood what he meant.

The circumstances were not uncommon: a guide was handy to point out the lies in the pool, the casts required were short and straightforward, and the choice of equipment and flies was guided by the experience of others. When the fly-fisher hooked a salmon it fought within the confines of a rather small pool, and the guide handtailed the fish. A little luck really was all it took to complete the job. This first-time salmon fisher may well have the chance to experience conditions offering a wider range of options and requiring more active decisions on his part. I've made the assumption that you will have few such advantages, other than previous fly-fishing experience, and are starting from scratch.

Atlantic salmon fishing is as much about the whole experience as it is about merely catching fish. It has to be, for the ordinary angler can wait several years before hooking and landing his first salmon. Only west-coast steelheaders and some saltwater big-game specialists share such a trying apprenticeship.

Of course, a novice, if a distant relative of King Midas, can also take a fish on his first cast. Witness the experience of a wonderful contemporary writer, Walt Wetherell. I would like to quote the entire text of ''The Bigger They Come'' from *Upland Stream* because no fly fisher should ever pass through life without having read at least one of Wetherell's stories, but my less-inspired version will have to do. On a family vacation in Nova Scotia, Walt and close kin walk to a secluded pool on the Cheticamp River. He has a little trout rod and prepares to angle for brookies with a number 14 Royal Wulff. A salmon leaps; he casts; the salmon rises; he strikes; the salmon is hooked; he plays, lands, and releases the salmon. No fooling, first cast ever on a salmon river!

Unhappily, too many newcomers and even a few old hands who should know better seem to be sliding into the selfish mentality of modern Western society. The creed of greed, grabbing one's share and that of others at all costs, is creeping like an oil slick along the banks of our rivers. Some say it's due to overcrowding, but I disagree. When I first came to the Miramichi River over twenty years ago there were small public pools that often accommodated several dozen anglers in a friendly and civilized manner. Now we find pre-dawn stakeout artists, pool hogs, snaggers, tag fillers, tail squeezers, trash droppers, rip-off commercial operators, and a variety of other louts about. The concept that parting with a license fee entitles one to take the limit — no matter how — is inimical to the survival of Atlantic salmon angling, particularly, but not exclusively, public fishing.

Because I believe that tradition is one of the cornerstones of civilized behavior and that knowledge of the past makes the present more interesting, you will find the history of the sport woven into the instructional cloth. Much of the written legacy comes from Britain, and so I make no apology for the frequent transatlantic references. Equally, however, I have tried to highlight the experiences and contributions of North American salmon anglers.

If I succeed in anything, I hope to convince you that respecting the codes and ethics of Atlantic salmon fishing, developed over many years for the pleasure of all, is the shortest route to a quality experience. To go further, if all you are interested in is catching fish, let me presume to advise the following: give this book to a friend, then arrange a trip to arctic Canada for northern pike. No waiting, minimum skill required, and lots of big, hard-fighting fish are virtually guaranteed.

Salmon (ASF photo)

Smolt and Parr (ASF photo)

CHAPTER 1

THE HABITS OF SALMON

A copse of aging elms crowned by the steel limbs of a hydro-electric tower blocked my view, but not the scent, of the new-mown hay. Nor did the elms muffle the monotonous chuckle of the tractor raking the hay into stacks. The Nashwaak River, sapped of its customary vigor by drought, sought to maintain a measure of respect by quarreling noisily with the stones blocking its downstream progress. I eavesdropped without attention while munching lunch on a rock stool permanently fixed at the point where the quarrel ended.

The sun had quartered the sky since I'd entered the water with damp streaks of early morning dew on my vest. Eight times the pool had suffered beneath the soles of my boots, and eight of my favorite flies had fondled its lies. For the last half hour of purposeful angling a White Wulff had floated repeatedly along twenty feet of what I call a special edge, rippling ten yards away — an edge where the current's fresher spirits gripped and invigorated the listless waters of a somnolent eddy. But now, reduced to a sodden conglomeration of white materials, the fly served only to amuse me as I flicked it repeatedly on ten feet of line into the streamy tendril curling around my feet.

Uncounted casts later, in full view, a grilse streaked across river from the special edge, grasped the fly firmly, and headed back. Bemused or befuddled by this nervy display, I did nothing. Halfway home the string ran out, it felt the hook and displayed its displeasure by leaping up to eye level and airmailing my fly.

Does this encounter deserve analysis? Well, for me it makes a statement about Atlantic salmon and angling for them. But let's preface my opinions with a bit of natural history.

Atlantic salmon spawn in their natal rivers in the fall. The eggs hatch the following spring and several months later the fry develop into parr. Now they look like small trout but with distinct vertical barring called, not surprisingly, parr marks. Feeding mostly on insects, they develop at a rate dependent on the fertility of the stream, and normally two to four years later are ready to go to sea. Just prior to departure, another spring event, parr acquire a silvery coating and become smolts.

Once at sea they follow migration paths unchanged for eons, feeding rapaciously and growing rapidly. The progeny of some rivers travel great distances while others remain closer to home. Now, one of nature's survival mechanisms asserts itself. Some salmon return to their birthplace, having spent only one winter in the ocean. These are the grilse. Others will remain at sea for two or more seasons before making the journey back home and rate the title salmon. (Hereafter, to avoid needless repetition, both salmon and grilse will be referred to as salmon unless a distinction is necessary.) The size of a salmon is directly related to the number of seasons spent in the ocean but nobody is certain what coded genetic instruction determines which ones will return while others stay. Certainly the nature of the river, height of falls, etc., will impose selection criteria and some rivers see only multi-sea winter fish.

Virtually without exception they ascend the river they left to begin the process anew. The few that stray are available to increase genetic diversity and restock rivers struck by natural or manmade disasters. Both grilse and salmon are fertile and even a macho male parr can be a daddy — although clearly less successfully than a full-grown buck.

Exactly when the salmon enter a stream and how quickly they move to spawning areas depends on pre-programming and water levels. A lack of water will often hold the migrants near the river mouth until conditions improve. With spring and fall being the favored seasons because of consistent water levels, some rivers see salmon entering either early or late while others get runs at both times. For example, the St. Mary's River in Nova Scotia gets most of its fish in May/June, whereas a hundred miles away, the Margaree River is noted for a run of big salmon in September/October. There are also a few streams blessed with fresh-run fish during the entire season. Variations in appearance and average size may be quite pronounced between runs in the same river and often the fish will be heading for different spawning areas.

Once in the river the salmon will move quickly if sufficient water is available but advance slowly and intermittently when conditions are less favorable. Natural obstacles may influence these movements significantly as, for example, a falls may only be passable when flows reach a particular volume. Salmon are very adaptable, and while wanting to reach the same patch of gravel from which they hatched, should conditions preclude this they will spawn over any satisfactory bottom. This isn't an efficient distribution of progeny over the suitable habitat but it beats wasting the journey.

After spawning, the salmon, now called kelts, drop back to the salt water immediately, or over-winter in the river and return to the ocean just after ice-out in the spring. A percentage of kelts regain their strength and return to spawn again — another survival tool. The proportion of multiple spawners varies from one river system to another but as an example, in the Miramichi River system in New Brunswick, the number in normal years is estimated to be 5 percent of the large salmon returns.

During the journey to the redd, or spawning beds, conventional wisdom says that the salmon don't feed. This has often been disputed by pointing out the fatal attraction of a worm (legal in certain parts of Great Britain) and instances where salmon rise like trout to a hatch of mayflies. I've watched the latter event several times (everybody says this is rare but everybody has seen it, so perhaps it's more frequent than we credit). My favorite analysis of this apparent conundrum was made by an eminent Scottish salmon biologist, who, after some period of discussion on the subject, is reported to have said with some pique, "salmon do not feed, but fortunately for you anglers, they do take food." While at first glance this statement meets all the requirements of an extended oxymoron, a little reflection reveals its perfection.

Salmon, in common with many other anadromous species, experience physiological changes prior to spawning, and the urge to procreate pushes other considerations aside. They have evolved the capacity to make the spawning run without requiring additional energy sources. However, they are low on the scale of evolution and so it can be expected that they would retain some vestige of the freshwater feeding pattern which is highly developed in parr. Equally, in Britain where they angle for fresh-run salmon in the cold water of January and February, many believe the success of large flies relates to sea-feeding memories.

This response to objects which approach their lies is, fortunately, individual in nature. I have seen salmon take bits of twigs and leaves, rise to seed puffballs, and chase minnows. I don't find this surprising. Experienced trout fishers will have encountered trout who take almost everything that drifts by into their mouths in order to assess its food value. Parr, who are in desperate competition for food, are no different. As adults, they are merely reacting, albeit irregularly, to this deeply imprinted instinct. Further, it makes sense that an object exhibiting signs of life is more likely to contain food value and is thus more attractive to an instinctive predator. Another argument put forward to support this position is that grilse, which are closer in time to the freshwater feeding pattern, are usually freer takers of a fly than the multi-sea winter salmon.

I don't wish to ride the legs out from under this hobby horse because, indisputably, at least some salmon will take an artificial fly. But how does all this relate to my reluctant grilse? Perhaps a hundred times that White Wulff floated right over the grilse's head and then as many more times it watched it drift submerged, thirty feet away. Individuality! Some salmon are simply a harder sell than others and in many cases they won't buy at all. But then that's the heart of the approach in this book — to get you to drum up prospects and hawk your wares.

CHAPTER 2

CONFORMATION OF A SALMON POOL

INTRODUCTION

Lies, not the little white ones you tell to sneak an afternoon's fishing but the places salmon stop during the journey to the spawning beds, are the mark of a salmon pool. If a section of water has them it's a pool; if it doesn't, it isn't. This is a bit confusing for trout fishermen who usually think like hydrologists, that is, a pool is deep, slow-moving water between fast-moving riffles.

Trout must feed to live, while salmon just hang around. Their needs are quite different. Salmon (often in small groups) select a comfortable spot out of the main current that supplies enough oxygen and cover. Rocks, depressions, ledges, edges (created where currents of different speed meet or where streams enter or merge), logs and eddies can qualify. Salmon have strong preferences at different water levels and a pool will usually be filled in a certain order. And it's the same order every year if the bottom has not changed. Why does one rock attract fish while an identical rock (to us) will not? No one knows. A general example of this variability is the run just upstream from Gray Rapids on the Main Southwest Miramichi River. In the early season the salmon hold nearer the left bank, while in the fall they move to the opposite side of the river.

Probably the most striking aspect of a salmon pool is the well-worn path leading to its bank, or else the number of anglers already wading its edges. Most pools you will fish are well known and marked on the river map you acquired (it is hoped) on or before your arrival. The trick of course is to find and cover the lies effectively.

THE BEND POOL

A good place to start is with the familiar bend pool represented in a typical configuration in Figure 1. The water enters at the head (A) after a stretch of fast water. The current races up against the far bank (B) while at the inside of the curve an area of gradually deepening slack water (C) begins. Often the inside of the bend has a sloping bottom of sand and gravel deposited there during high water. The exposed gravel (D) is called shingle.

On the outside of the bend the current gradually slows but usually maintains a good flow. The central current (E) slows down even more as the depth increases. Next the bottom begins to slope upward as the pool opens into the tail area (F). The tail is normally of a more uniform depth across the river and the current gradually

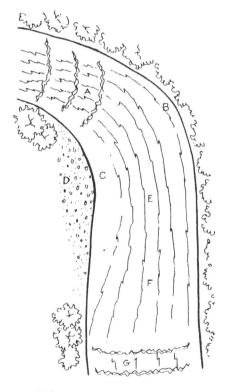

FIGURE 1. Bend Pool

picks up speed prior to breaking over at the lip (G) into the next stretch of fast water. Depending on the time of day, water levels, etc., all these areas can hold salmon (although those on the shingle are likely to feel seriously out of sorts). In any event, depending on the size of the river, bend pools may occupy a hundred feet to a quarter of a mile or more.

THE RUN

A run is a straight section of river where the flow is relatively uniform between the banks. The bottom slopes gradually downward from the shoreline to the middle. The gradient is moderate and constant. Some runs peter out in pools, others lead into riffles. A gravel bar, pushed up by the currents or spring ice, in the middle of a wide portion of a big river often creates a superb run. The bar forces most of the flow, and the salmon, between itself and one bank.

Fish can be found in favored lies throughout a run. Only experience with a particular stretch under a variety of water conditions will let you find these lies with any degree of certainty. Nonetheless, surface swirls indicating a larger than average rock are always good bets. Bill Ensor, an experienced New Brunswick salmon addict, suggests that early in the season you should keep an eye open for fresh eel nests which show up as white patches on the bottom. He has often located salmon lying in these shallow depressions.

THE BOGAN

When a stream (or spring) cuts a deep, slow-moving channel across a river's floodplain to join the main flow, you have a bogan. At least you do in New Brunswick (backwaters are also called bogans, but unless I indicate otherwise I mean the stream or spring type when using the word). Because the stream is usually cooler than the river, such places are extremely important, particularly in summer. When the temperature of the river closes in on lethal levels (around 80 degrees F.), salmon regularly move into bogans. They stack up in great numbers and become very unsettled. Many riparian owners sensibly close these areas to fishing to prevent harassment and the ever-present danger of foul hooking. In some instances the Canadian Department of Fisheries and Oceans may take over such decision-making for the entire river system by issuing variation orders to close the spring bogans to fishing.

Figure 2 is a rough sketch of one such pool on the Main Southwest Miramichi River. It has another interesting (explainable in complicated fluid mechanics' jargon) but not unique characteristic in that the fast current over the gravel has formed a shallow dropoff, cutting diagonally across the river (B). In times of plenty, salmon can be found nosed up to the dropoff (B), along the special edge (A) where the two flows meet, or in the deep, slow-moving water

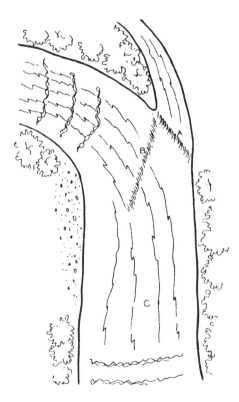

FIGURE 2. Bogan

at the end of the riffle (C). The latter is considered excellent dry fly water. Several years ago, while fishing during a terrible drought with John Randolph of *Fly Fisherman* magazine, we were invited to try a similar pool by its owners, Alex and Vicki Mills of Olde River Lodge. Casting about six feet into the bogan and letting the fly work the edge at A, I picked up a small grilse, a welcome bit of action.

THE LEDGE POOL

Ledge pools are formed where a slate ledge ends out in the river, producing a sharp drop-off. They also occur where the river runs hard against a rock face and has carved a step below the water line.

Salmon find the edge of the ledge a great lie because it provides excellent cover and shade as well as a layer of slower-moving water. They will stack up in these locations and stay for long periods. Gilvert van Ryckevorsel, a renowned underwater photographer of salmon, has taken many of his best shots in ledge pools.

THE PLUNGE POOL

Plunge pools are formed below waterfalls and can be very deep. Salmon congregate in these areas waiting for a certain height or flow of water that will let them surmount the obstacle. I have had minimal exposure to such locations, but in the ones visited the salmon tend to mill about the pool and are difficult to take. They will also lie facing downriver in back eddies formed beside both shores.

There is a pint-sized falls on the LaHave River in Nova Scotia flowing into a large pool. During several visits I found salmon swimming slowly around this pond. Everything in my box, including tiny trout flies, was uniformly rejected. Plenty of other anglers had had a go at these impatient travelers, which may have contributed to their utter contempt for my efforts.

STILLWATERS AND RELATIVES

Rivers winding through lowlands may have extensive stretches of very slow flow. Often called deadwaters or stillwaters, the water is usually dark and unattractive and the bottom muddy. Salmon will cruise if the current is too slow for comfort; otherwise they are usually found in deep water near the bottom. Ponds in the headwaters of some otherwise fast-paced rivers are similar in nature but with potential lies near inlets and outlets.

True lakes breaking up sections of a salmon river are less common in North America than in Britain, but there are enough of them to warrant a mention. They seldom resemble ponds or deadwaters because the bottom may be sandy, rocky, or weedy and the water quite clear. Salmon invariably cruise around the shoreline and can be very tough to interest.

TIDAL POOLS

Another area that can prove interesting is the brackish water pool(s) where a small river runs into the salt. The currents in these pools reverse with the tide, and particularly when low-water conditions keep the salmon from entering the river, they may move in and out with the tide. Proper timing could result in a bonanza.

THE NON-POOL POOL

Between well-known pools are sections of broken water. While these bits don't look attractive, you can find salmon there. I speculate as follows: 1) During a heavy run all the favored lies in a pool may be occupied. This pushes salmon out into less-favored locations. 2) A fish may get caught moving between pools, particularly during low water. In these conditions salmon are loathe to cross the shallow water at the lip of a pool or enter a thin riffle in daylight and so may drop back to a lie in the broken water (occasionally called grilse holes), until evening arrives.

One day I finished working a small bend pool on an unfamiliar section of the Dungarvon River in New Brunswick and decided to walk downstream to the camp pool by way of the river instead of taking the normal path through the woods. Moving along, I noticed an area of dark water, a sort of trench, in what was otherwise a fairly uninteresting stretch of shallow, fast riffle. Having been summoned for lunch I didn't take a cast, but over the meal I asked the assembled if anyone had had any success there in the past. The answer was ''no.''

The next day I took the same route and ran a fly along the trench but without result. But someone had listened to my comment because early the following morning, on his way back from checking the upper pools, one of the party decided to give the spot a go and picked up an eight-pound salmon. Sometimes it's the early bird . . . ! I doubt that fish would have stayed there long before pushing forward to the pool just above.

CHAPTER 3

WET-FLY TACTICS

INTRODUCTION

Controlling the depth and speed of a subsurface fly as it passes in front of a visible fish or suspected lie is at the heart of all wet-fly methods. Happily, the salmon have yet to release to their acolytes a universal formula for predicting their preferences. I say "happily" because the arrival streamside of the pocket computer, depth sounder, and velocimeter would put a golf club in my hands instead. Yet, not all is left to chance, for in the words of Tennyson, ". . . experience is an arch wherthro' gleams that untravell'd world." And so, with time, anglers develop a sense of when the fly is swimming seductively. Does this mean neophytes won't catch fish? To the contrary, the river often collects an unmanaged cast and serves the fly to a salmon as irresistibly as it offers a dun to a rising brown.

In North America, controlling depth by weighting the fly is forbidden. The options are varying: a) the type of line, b) casting techniques, or c) the size of the fly. Speed is altered by changing the direction of the cast and/or line manipulations. What follows are methods of presenting the wet fly to control its speed and depth. To orient you, the left bank is the one on your left-hand side when you are facing downriver.

THE CLASSIC METHOD

About a half mile above Gray Rapids, the Miramichi River spans several hundred feet of the valley floor. Thirty feet up the steep slopes, birch and spruce trees bear the scars of spring ice encounters. The current is uniform, locally disturbed by subsurface rocks as the bottom slopes upward near the banks. Particularly in the fall, salmon occupy lies within casting distance of the right bank. We cast out at a forty-degree angle downstream (the angle varies slightly with current speed) and let the fly sweep into the shore. This is the classic method of fishing for Atlantic salmon with a wet fly.

Why "classic method"? That's because it was the original style of fly-fishing for salmon, albeit with a sunk line, and remains the most efficient means of covering the water when you can't see the fish. The line is straight and the fly is allowed to move across the stream under the influence of the current, finishing up directly below the angler. After the fly touches down, hold the rod parallel to the surface, or tilted slightly upward if wading deep, and follow the swing of the fly with the rod tip.

If the current is uniform, the fly is normally left to its own devices while swinging. Adjusting it by hand or rod movements is out. But rules in salmon fishing are as flexible as Jello; Robert Pashley, a notable British angler, attributed his stunning successes on the Wye River to a trembling hand. Also, as we will see in the following section, the "classic method" needs plenty of help when forced to deal with jumbled currents.

A straight cast does not imply, as some people suggest, that the line, leader, and fly will remain in a perfectly straight line. All the little pushes and pulls of the current and line inevitably create a curve in the leader. Such a serendipitous result of the physics of the process is more than we deserve. It frees our designer-dressed model to flaunt her charms as she swings across the runway. Robert Hartman, writing in *About Fishing* (1935), put it engagingly: "A salmon fly should never look bored." Of course, when the cast is completed and the fly is at the dangle, all is straight once more. Leave the fly hanging for a moment or two in case a salmon has followed it in, then gather the shooting line in slow strips and take a step downstream in preparation for the next cast.

Begin at the head of the pool and repeat the cast-and-step procedure until reaching the end of the fishable water. The result, depending on the size of the pool and the angler's abilities, is that the fly will pass over, or close to, all the lies. It is a very efficient searching strategy which also lets several anglers fish the pool in an orderly fashion.

The Swallow Bank Pool mentioned in text

On an intermediate line — Margaree River

Let's return for a moment to the earlier statement that control of depth and speed of the fly is paramount. Obviously, line selection affects just what control we can exert over the path of the fly. Consequently, while still referring to the classic method and its basic modifications, I choose to deal with floating and sinking lines in separate sections.

THE FLOATING LINE

Bright salmon fishing in North America is widely restricted to the period between late spring and early fall. The water is normally both warm and low enough to use a floating line effectively. And when moving at the "right" speed, the floating line keeps the fly swimming just under the surface.

Figure 3 has the angler in a common situation, on the right bank. Right-handers usually find it easier to cast from this side. The cast is made as indicated and allowed to swim undisturbed to the bank. In the illustration the stream flow increases uniformly toward the end of the cast, making adjustments of the line on the water unnecessary.

An error often made by inexperienced anglers, and occasionally by those who should know better, is to attempt to cast beyond their range. The usual result of overreaching is that the end of the line and the leader are piled up at the end of the cast (see Figure 4).

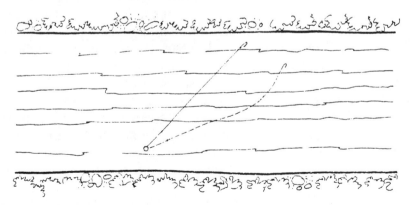

FIGURE 3. Small Hook in Cast

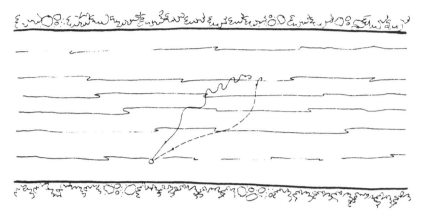

FIGURE 4. Pileup and result

The current begins to act immediately on the belly of the line and it starts to move across stream. In the time it takes to straighten out the coils, a sharp curve develops in the terminal tackle. Suddenly the fly is pulled at high speed across stream until the current sorts things out. Often this won't be until the end of the swing. Another drawback to a "bird's nest" is that for a time after the fly lands it is sinking and drifting downstream out of control, drifting not swimming. This is usually undesirable, although there are techniques, discussed further on, for fishing a wet fly dead drift under exceptional circumstances.

Many rivers fished by wading are quite small. At the head of the pool, the length of line needed to cover the entire river is comfortably within your capabilities. Moving downstream the river widens, the current slows, and the water deepens. If you continue to try and reach the far bank it's likely you'll reach a position where your casts land on the water looking like the wires behind your stereo. Stop, wind in a little line and continue to fish under control for the remainder of the pool. Regardless of a visceral belief that the fish are always lying tight to the far bank, it isn't so. If inconsiderate companions are plucking salmon from beyond your controllable range, and you are very sure of where the deed is actually being done, then give it your best shot. Perhaps you'll be lucky.

Even if you can make cookies without butter, they taste better with the real thing. The ability to throw a long line and cope with the big brothers of pleasant summer zephyrs is a salmon fisher's secret to better baking. Practice, and coaching from a qualified instructor if available, will make your angling more enjoyable and productive.

Late one October afternoon I reached an instructive pool on the Margaree River. The fast current at the head clung tightly to the steep right-hand bank, its gravel slope pocked with swallow nests. I could see that continuing downstream would run me into a deep bit of slack water which, combined with the current speed, would upset the swing of the fly (in the photo, the slack water can be seen on the left). To beat the problem I took several steps sideways into the run and kept casting at a shallow angle until the whole line was out. About half way down, just before the fly reached the edge of the slack water, came the take. The eighteen-pound female tore off downstream for a quarter mile before I caught up and worked her to shore.

Another way to achieve almost the same effect as a long, shallow-angle cast is to make a reach cast. This involves moving the rod and line up and out over the stream before the forward cast is completed. By following the line downstream with the rod and feeding some slack line from your left hand, you effectively reduce the angle of the line on the water (see Figure 5). Notice that I said, "almost the same effect." Because the reach cast involves

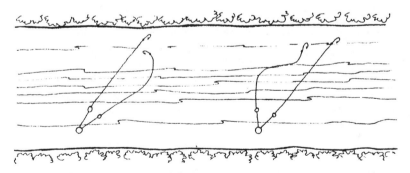

FIGURE 5. Reach Cast

some downstream drifting motion of the fly, the swing won't be identical to that of the sharper-angle cast. The effectiveness of the reach is also influenced by the length of line thrown. The longer the cast, the lower the proportion of the line that is aerially re-positioned.

I find it interesting that although this "cast" was popularized in North America by Doug Swisher during the last twenty years, it was common practice among British salmon fishers in the thirties. Frederick Hill mentions it almost offhandedly in his 1948 book *Salmon Fishing*, written after he retired. He wrote, "Cast slowly, shooting the usual few yards of line, watch the cast and fly going out to their mark; immediately the line straightens out and when the fly is about two yards from the water, give the rod point a quiet, upward lift, in the direction required. This will make a perfect mend, ready to fish straight away." Although he calls it a mend, it's a reach to us.

Mending is the most important floating line-control technique. A mend in North American parlance is simply relocating a portion of the line which is already on the water. Sadly, considerable misinformation abounds about just what can be accomplished with a mend. Take the case of a sixty-foot cast crossing a swift center current. Left alone the line will develop a severe downstream bow (position 2 in Figure 6). This will cause the fly to speed up and follow an erratic path. You may hear that you can lift that extensive curve, right down to the leader, and place it upstream to posi-

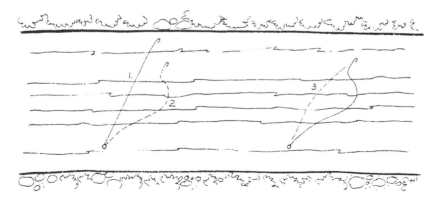

FIGURE 6. Mend

tion 3 in the figure without moving the fly. Donkey dust! Even if
it were theoretically possible, which I doubt, the precision control
of the applied force necessary to pull this off is beyond the
capabilities of anyone.

The situation changes if there are some squiggles in the line
outboard of the curve that can absorb this motion, as in the case
of an up-and-across slack-line trout cast. You can also deal with
a swift current close to the rod by frequent small mends without
affecting the fly.

Originally, in Britain, mending was accomplished by simply
lifting and re-positioning the line. And a lot of it moved when the
angler gripped a twenty-foot rod. To mend the line with our half-
pint sticks, use a semi-circular motion of the arm and wrist to flip
the curve in the line upstream. A slight downstream movement
of the rod at the beginning can assist in freeing the close-in line
from the drag of the current. This seems easy but requires practice. A weight-forward line increases the difficulty because the light
running line has trouble moving the heavy forward section.
However, with time you will learn to control the amount of line
moved and to disturb the fly as little as possible. And, as your skill
increases, you will be able to throw some slack line held in the left
hand into the mend during the motion, providing additional time
before the offensive curve reforms.

Suppose that between you and the faster-flowing stream there
is a stretch of slower or dead water. As the line swings toward the
bank, a hinge will develop at the junction of the fast and slow currents. This prevents the fly from swimming smoothly through the
edge between the currents. All that's necessary to correct this is
a delicate downstream mend. Also, you can occasionally resurrect
a bad cast by a vigorous upstream mend which straightens the
leader and, while altering the swim of the fly, allows you to maintain contact and control. A minor point to mention here — I fish
out my bad casts. I don't like seeing anyone rip a line from the
middle of the river.

Although the material is unsteady in other areas, I enjoy Robert
Hartman's comments about mending in *About Fishing* (1935): ''In
theory and in a diagram this mending of the line presents no difficulties. In practice it is otherwise. For the life of me I can't remove
the belly without jerking the fly. . . . No doubt by the time that
I am too old and too rheumaticky to fish I shall have acquired the
knack. Meanwhile I persevere.'' Yes!

Then there is the problem of a fly moving too slowly. This can happen in the middle of a pool or in a very wide tail-out area. Increase the fly's speed by making a downstream mend, or cast more directly across stream (subject to room for the backcast), both of which will cause the current to apply more force to the line. Another method of increasing fly speed is to lead the fly strongly with the rod and continue the sweep until the rod is pointing directly inshore.

After much effort to convince you that controlling the speed of the fly is important, it grieves me to admit that other methods are sometimes successful. Not long ago, I met an angler who casts directly across stream no matter what the current and doesn't bother to mend the line. He catches too many salmon to be dismissed out of hand. Despite that, my results when I've tried this in fast currents would entitle me to file for protection under the bankruptcy statutes.

There is also a middle road. Percy Laming, one of the first anglers to use a floating line and small flies for salmon fishing, was prepared to let the line get downstream of the fly. He cast more across than down and let the current put a hook in the line to move the fly swiftly in front of a salmon or a known lie. But the critical component in all this was that Laming fished according to the water, adjusting the angle and length of line to land the fly close to a salmon and to yield the swim he wanted. In *Fine and Far Off* (1952), Jock Scott called this the dragging-fly technique.

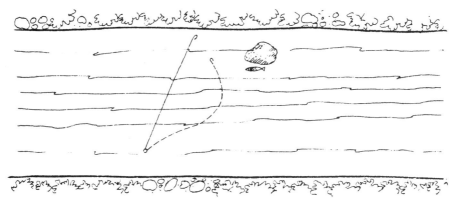

FIGURE 7. Percy Laming Technique

THE SINKING LINE

The spare spool filled with some form of sinking line comes out of the back of your vest when the height, color, or temperature of the water dictate a closer presentation to a lie. A long-surviving tenet of salmon fishing is that the colder the water the slower the fly should swim and the closer it should pass to the fish. One cool October morning at Sky Lodge pool on the Margaree River, I stood around snapping pictures while Joe Garman, using an intermediate line, outfished a number of other experienced anglers casting floaters with the same fly.

I'm not a big fan of intermediate lines because of a bad habit of dropping some shooting line on the water — making for short shoots! But, and it could be a big ''but,'' some excellent anglers believe that a fully submerged line is less likely to unsettle salmon than a floating line — particularly when the sun is out. Cliff Brown, who taught me how to fish for salmon, liked to have the end of his line dirty enough to sink a bit. He believed it fished the fly a little deeper and that this was more attractive. I'm sure he didn't realize that he was following in the footsteps of the great angler Percy Laming, who left the last several feet of his line ungreased. Is it possible that reduced line visibility was the real reason for their successes?

Super-fast sinkers, while legal, are unsportsmanlike in my view, particularly when used over visible salmon holding in deep pools, and are no better than using leaded flies. In concert with the large irons favored under high-water conditions they are too apt to foul-hook fish. This is an abomination; there are sleazy operators, not sportsmen, who strip these outfits in with small jerks, ''just to keep the fly from snagging on the bottom!''

A sink-tip, intermediate, or slow-sinking line can be matched to the conditions. The sink-tip allows you to mend and control the floating portion; the intermediate and slow sinkers let you get in one immediate mend. I have pretty well dispensed with the latter two in my fishing and substituted tapered braided sinking leaders (discussed in detail in Chapter 6). You, however, may be able to handle forty or fifty feet of shooting line coiled in your hand (or be unconventional enough to wear a shooting basket). In which case, intermediate or slow-sinking lines may be used to advantage.

Additional depth can be achieved by casting more upstream or increasing the size of the fly, sometimes to 4/0! Meathooks like these are not recommended for inexperienced anglers, except for those with very hard heads. Reach casts will also help to slow the fly down and gain additional control.

OTHER WET FLY METHODS

Greased Line

Only the sky retained its color as sunset robbed the spruce trees on the far bank of the Little Southwest Miramichi of their individuality. A fishless day was fading away as I stood on a shifting shingle bar in the middle of the river. Thirty yards further on, the placid tailwaters of the pool became agitated by a riffle. But I was more concerned with the swirling midstream currents just below me and the submerged rock they betrayed. Staring at the tranquil slot trapped between turbulent edges, I felt a salmon's presence.

Previous down-and-across casts from upstream had pulled the fly erratically through the eddy, so I cast straight out and mended line vigorously several times to bring the fly as smoothly as possible into and out of the lie. On the second cast the size 6 Cosseboom took hold. The salmon was lost when it uncharacteristically swam full tilt toward me, but the lesson of its transient capture by the greased-line method wasn't forgotten.

Today, "greased line" identifies an angling technique. But this wasn't always true. During the early development of dry-fly tactics for trout, anglers kept fly and line floating by false casting to shed excess moisture. Someone soon realized that applying water-repellent substances to the line would keep it up, hence, "greased line." Then, in the waning years of the nineteenth century, Percy Laming and others began catching salmon during summer conditions with the floating-line/small-fly combination.

The term "greased-line fishing" is now associated with the style developed by A.H.E. Wood early in this century. For some thirty years his salmon fishing was largely confined to Cairnton on the Aberdeenshire Dee in the west of Scotland — although the genesis of the method was catching several Irish salmon by "dibbling" a

White Moth trout fly over their heads and giving slack after the take. Dibbling was centuries old (and still works today) but Wood was stimulated to modify and expand its application.

Wood wrote sparingly, leaving it largely to others to interpret his methods for popular consumption. Crawford Little, in *The Great Salmon Beats*, summed up the unfortunate result with, ''And yet, what a host of misinterpretation it has been subjected to, time after time after time.'' However, Wood's words are available. He was interviewed for the 1926 anthology *Fisherman's Pie*, edited by W.A. Hunter, approved notes on the method for Hardy's 1926 catalog, left considerable private correspondence, and wrote a chapter for The Lonsdale Library volume *Salmon Fishing* (1935). But these fragments would not become the bible. Particularly for postwar anglers, the definitive text is *Greased Line Fishing* by Jock Scott, first published circa 1936.

Let's begin by quoting from that text: ''The basic idea is to use the line as a float for, and controlling agent of, the fly; to suspend the fly just beneath the surface of the water, and to control its path in such a way that it swims diagonally down and across the stream, entirely free from the slightest pull on the line.'' More than anything else, it's those last nine words that have caused all the trouble. What's worse, they have frequently been summarized to read, ''without drag.'' The phrase is nonsense. A wet fly swimming without pull from the line is heading downstream with the current and will shortly (how shortly will depend on its weight) sink to the bottom. It must act under the pull of the line if it's to move across stream. A closer reading of what Wood says later in the text almost clarifies the situation. He seemed to be saying that you must keep the line upstream of the fly. Unfortunately, there are so many contradictory statements in his correspondence that you wonder if he ever really did have a firm grip on what the fly was doing. In Figure 7 I've tried to give what I believe to be the essence of the method.

Why did Wood want to cast across stream with a floating line? The speculation is that he didn't like wading and wanted to use shorter than normal (at that time) single-handed rods. A.J. Barry, his personal friend and correspondent, wrote in an appendix to *The Floating Line for Salmon and Sea Trout* (1939) by Anthony Crossley,

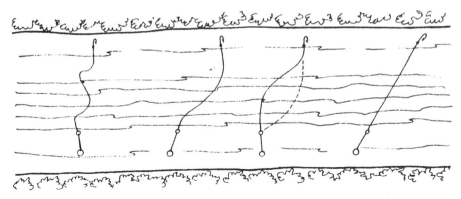

FIGURE 8. Greased Line

"You will notice the reason why he (Wood) never fished with a double-handed rod, which was simply that he was unable to throw any sort of line with one. . . ." So, to cover the water from his bank and apply the Irish lesson of keeping the fly near the surface, the solution was virtually ordained.

Several modern writers have suggested that Wood wasn't advocating casts directly across or upstream but simply more upstream than is currently popular. Although substantiated by identical drawings in *Salmon Fishing* and *Greased Line Fishing*, this theory is contradicted by his words. In *Fisherman's Pie* he says, ". . . but my fly is very often floating or just awash, especially during the first portion of the cast. If the water is suitable I cast across and slightly up-stream, leaving slack line and letting the fly drift down until the line begins to tighten; during most of this time the fly will be floating and I often get fish at that part of the cast. When the line tightens the fly will go under water, but as the line and part of the cast are still floating, the fly is only just under the water." The Hardy's catalog, moreover, even specifies an angle of 25 degrees upstream. Before continuing with Wood's methods, it may be worthwhile to fill in a little background because his time was when most modern methods were developed. Atlantic salmon fishing in Britain is largely a Scottish affair. Early in the century the best runs were in late winter or early spring, and the icy waters dictated a large and deeply fished fly. This suited the sinking lines of the period. Once the water warmed and levels dropped, the salmon rejected these tactics, so many beats were abandoned or leased for much less money until the fall run appeared. Persistent summertime anglers offered sacrifices of worms and prawns.

Wood received considerable attention because he offered a successful way to dispense with bait (and coincidentally increase the value of summer leases). But his was not the only path to a better life. Alexander Grant, a formidable angler, cast the equivalent of a modern intermediate line (heavily oiled silk) prodigious distances (120 to 140 feet) at a shallow downstream angle. This presentation fished small flies at a uniform speed and close to the surface. Another celebrated salmon fisher, Ernest Crosfield, threw a sunk line across stream and stripped the fly in quickly to keep it near the surface. Percy Laming's floating line techniques were mentioned earlier.

Back to Wood's methods. To cast across or upstream and then control the fly's speed (read, slow down, in most circumstances), it's necessary to mend. Some say Wood invented the technique, but they are wrong. Major John P. Traherne, in *Fishing* (1885), wrote: "There is a way of taking the belly out of a line, which was taught me by an old fisherman when fishing the Kirkcudbrightshire Dee in my younger days. I dare say many of my readers will recollect old Jemmie Gordon, professional salmon fisherman. . . . It was Jemmie who pointed out to me the evil of allowing a belly to remain in my line, and who taught me how to rectify it." There follows a diagram and description of what is unmistakably mending. To be fair, Wood may have been the first to employ multiple mends with a floating line.

To contribute to the controlled movement of the fly, Wood suggested that the caster lead the line slightly with the rod. As pointed out in the section on the "classic method," this lets the fly drop downstream a bit while swinging across, thus increasing the time it takes to get to the near bank. Ostensibly, the fly should pass somewhat broadside to the fish. In Wood's words, "Perhaps the chief point is that you can control the angle the fly swims in the water. I prefer the fly to be at an angle of, say, 60 degrees." This is a touch rich! A fly is subject to all the vagaries of the current unless very strongly led.

A lightly dressed fly, at a time when many were still using full dressed "classics" was also an integral part of the system, but Wood was certainly no pattern junkie. Blue Charm, Silver Blue, and March Brown sparsely tied in a wide range of sizes were sufficient. He even experimented successfully with undressed painted hooks.

Wood realized, partly from his original Irish experience, that if one strikes upon seeing a rise to a fly swimming near the surface, many salmon will be missed. Throughout his writings he vacillated over how to give the fish time to fully grab the fly. From time to time he suggested feeding slack line held in the hand as soon as a rise was spotted, but almost as often he advised doing nothing except tightening up. I believe he altered his tactics depending on the strength of the current. Look for more on this question in Chapter 9.

Wood's final dictum was not to fish with the greased line unless the air is warmer than the water. This is similar to the homily that time spent on the river before the morning mist lifts is time wasted. I suspect this idea has more to do with the angler's desire for a late breakfast than with salmon behavior.

What role is the greased line method to be assigned in the modern salmon angler's arsenal, particularly in North America? In my opinion, it's when we are fully exploiting the dry fly/damp fly characteristics of Bombers and Buck Bugs (covered in more depth in the next chapter) that we owe the greatest debt to the ideas of A.H.E. Wood. Skillful use under most conditions depends on your ability to mend delicately, especially substantial lengths of line, a facility which can only be acquired through practice. The shorter rods, weight-forward lines, and wading approach favored in North America make these long mends difficult. For most anglers this restricts the application of the original technique to casts under sixty feet.

THE PATENT

Occasionally misunderstood, the Patent as first practiced is nothing more than dry fly fishing with a large, hairy, wet fly. It's originator, Colonel L.S. Thompson, had great success on the Restigouche using flies developed by A.S. Trude. Colonel Bates, in *Atlantic Salmon Flies and Fishing*, suggests that the technique is improved by using a sinking or sink tip line, although I believe these lines would make life difficult. The concept is to attract a salmon by simulating life with motion of the mobile dressing as opposed to the swimming movements of the fly. Essential to the success of this method when the fly is sunk is a good view of the fish so one can see the take and time the strike.

Jean-Paul Dube suggests, in his book *Salmon Talk* (1983), that even on the Restigouche and surrounding waters, the Patent has only a few diehard adherents. He believes the salmon have sworn off large flies. And the flies were huge by today's summer standards, rarely falling below 3/0. Red and Silver Abbeys, the Fiery Brown, the Grizzley King, and Rats, all tied with bucktail wings, were among the favorites.

The method is rarely applicable to shared public waters, particularly upstream since it interferes with the person fishing behind you. It can, however, be practiced across or downstream by using slack-line casts. If exploited with a sunk fly/floating line, some type of indicator will greatly assist in detecting takes and you must also strike immediately.

NYMPHING

Closely associated with the Patent method is the upstream nymph technique of trout fishing. One major restriction, the illegality of adding any weight to the fly or leader, reduces its effectiveness for salmon angling. Still, it has outstanding potential under certain circumstances. When a salmon has been located in two or three feet of water and has resisted the best of your dry fly charms, bend on a number 10 natural-looking nymph tied on a stout wire hook. Add an indicator to the leader about a foot farther from the fly than the depth of the water (although beware, the silly fish may rise to the indicator after refusing your artistic dries).

Now make an experimental cast off to the side to check how far above the fish you must cast to put the nymph on its nose. Then it's time for a business cast. Watch the indicator like a hawk. As it may be necessary to put the fly practically in the salmon's mouth, don't be discouraged until you're sure the drift has been thoroughly covered. A discreet observer can help ensure that the nymph is really tickling the fish. It is possible to foul-hook a salmon with this technique, something no sportsman does on purpose.

Edward Hewitt told in *A Trout and Salmon Fisherman for Seventy Five Years* (1948) of using true nymph patterns for salmon in the 1920's or earlier. It appears that he preferred to fish them downstream with movement. Although not calling it by name, his technique at times was the same as the induced-rise tactic of trout fishing, where the angler attempts to have the fly rise like a hatching insect immediately in front of the fish.

THE RIFFLING HITCH

Portland Creek, a famous Newfoundland river, was the birthplace of this method. Lee Wulff popularized its use. The story goes that local fishermen, in order to re-use the flies with broken or brittle gut eyes left behind as "tips" by visiting British naval officers, knotted their leaders behind the head. This resulted in the leader protruding at right angles from the hook, causing the fly to skim or riffle the surface as it came across stream. It turns a normal wet fly into a waking fly, like a Bomber or other similar design.

Today, after a wet fly is knotted to the leader, one or two half hitches are thrown behind its head (Figure 9 shows a single hitch). The leader should come out on the opposite side of the fly from the side of the river you are fishing. That is, looking at the eye of the fly, the leader should emerge from the left side when fishing the right bank, and vice versa. Though successful on some Newfoundland streams, the method is less popular elsewhere — although west coast steelheaders adore it. I've never caught a fish this way although I can hardly be said to have given it a fair trial, using it only a few times as a last resort.

BACKING UP THE POOL

Restricted to solitary confinements, this technique was developed in the United Kingdom. With the aim of swimming a fly

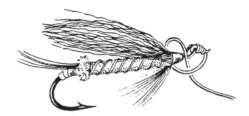

FIGURE 9. Riffle Hitch

upstream over the lies, you start at the end of a pool and, after making a cast down and across, back up slowly until the fly reaches the dangle. Repeat this until you reach the head of the pool or until the fly begins to fish too quickly.

You'd better be sure the footing is clear of obstructions or you'll find yourself drying out in a chiropractor's office. Another drawback is that the salmon sees the line before the fly, but since it's unusual to back up before fishing down, this probably has little effect. Opportunities to use this technique are likely to be few and far between on public waters in North America, but occasionally a deadwater area beyond where most anglers leave the pool may be suitable.

MOVING THE FLY

Adding movement to a nicely swinging fly, be it pulsing with the rod or twitching with the line hand, has its share of devotees. The old hands who got me past my greenhorn phase were tough on ruining a natural swim, so I can offer little guidance. If there is insufficient current to move the fly at an attractive speed, for example in stillwaters, something must be done. And a reluctant salmon should be exposed to every variation you can muster. The only legitimate advice is to experiment.

BOATS

"Fishing the drop" from a boat is the standard method used to cover salmon holding in a body of water that is too large or otherwise unsuitable for wading. Normally canoes are used because they can negotiate shallow waters and are responsive in rapids to the skilled touch of an expert with a set pole. The goal is to show the fly to all possible fish in the stretch.

Start by anchoring at the head of the pool and then casting a short line alternatively on either side of the boat. After each throw the angler pulls about three feet of additional line off the reel until reaching the limits of his casting capabilities. At that point the line is wound in, the anchor pulled, and the canoe allowed to drift downriver about three quarters of the distance of the longest cast. The procedure then begins again. The fly should be worked for a few minutes at the end of each cast because, unlike a wader whose fly usually finishes the swing in shallow water, the boat angler's fly is still very much alive.

In almost all circumstances (except in very large rivers), once a salmon is hooked, the angler is put ashore to carry on the fight. The obvious advantages are a stable platform and ease of movement. Should the salmon try to take the fisherman on a trip downstream where following is impossible because of the terrain, the boat can be re-boarded for the chase.

AFTER-ALL

Beyond technique is the special character of downstream wet fly fishing for salmon. There is a feeling of well being, a joining with the river when moving with the current that is lost when bracing its flow. In smaller rivers there is no need to false cast; a simple pick-up and shoot on the forward cast covers the water, and a satisfying rhythm soon develops. With experience the subconscious watches the swing of the fly and a habitually busy brain is freed for repose, submerged in the pulse and breath of the living river.

CHAPTER 4

THE DRY FLY

In the late afternoon of a sunny summer's day, the Miramichi River takes on the appearance of anemic molasses flecked with thousands of flashing diamonds. Years ago at such a time, I met an angler fishing my brother's water at Gray Rapids Lodge. Salmon were moving over the bar about thirty feet upriver and some forty feet from shore. After hurried introductions the stranger detached a decoration from his hatband, rubbed it with Mucilin floatant, and dropped it in my hand. "Put on this Bug," he said, although its clipped deer hair body wound with hackle looked like no insect I'd ever seen, "and cast it up on the bar letting it float back dead drift." I did as I was told. Within a couple of feet the surface bulged and I hooked my first salmon on a dry fly.

BEGINNINGS

Although the English claim to be the first to angle for salmon with a dry fly — on the Test with an imitation mayfly in 1906 — I consider the claim forfeit due to their failure to develop the technique (a rough example of "use it or lose it"). The continuous history of dry-fly fishing for salmon unfolded on Canadian rivers, beginning with Colonel Monell's successes on the Upsalquitch River in New Brunswick around 1914. George LaBranche, who became the technique's foremost early champion, recorded the Upsalquitch experiments in his book *The Dry Fly and the Salmon* (1924). According to LaBranche, Monell's first dry-fly salmon came to a No. 12 Whirling Dun, an English trout fly. The equally well-known Edward Hewitt makes a claim of an independent, but undated, discovery while fishing in Newfoundland. Certainly he participated in the early development, as a good friend and frequent companion of Monell and LaBranche. The idea seems to have traveled quick-

Captive of a dry — North Pole Brook, N.B.

Dry Fly Water — slow water near tail (Bill Ensor photo)

ly; by 1927 Bliss Perry reported, in *Pools and Ripples*, discussions of the quality of dry-fly rods for salmon during a trip to the Miramichi in a manner that suggests they weren't a novelty. And in the same year, Frank Parker Day in *The Autobiography of a Fisherman* wrote that a cinnamon sedge is the best dry fly for the Tusket River in Nova Scotia.

It was LaBranche who visited A.H.E. Wood in the summer of 1925 and attempted to catch salmon on a dry fly in the Scottish Dee and a few other rivers. He rose many fish but had trouble hooking them. By this time LaBranche had developed a series of heavily hackled salmon dry flies (Figure 10) based on his observations that a high-floating artificial was the most effective. Although Wood and others attributed the failure to the flies, the performer disagreed. He believed it had more to do with the low-water conditions, the gallery assembled on the far bank, and his being out of practice. The widespread reporting of the debacle did little to advance the dry fly's prospects in Great Britain.

In 1962, Lee Wulff made the journey to Scotland for a friendly contest with Donald Rudd (Jock Scott). Wulff had better "luck" and won with a single salmon taken on a dry fly. He later caught several more on the Dee, proving that the dry fly works on either side of the pond.

LaBranche had a fascination with what I've called earlier "the special edge." He termed it "the groove" or "the sacred inch"

FIGURE 10. LaBranche Dry Fly

and insisted that floating a dry fly precisely along this separation of currents was essential. He carefully noted that this was far more important for large salmon, as grilse were often tempted to rush the fly from a distance. Another of his observations was that salmon refused flies dragging downstream but would occasionally come to those moving slower than the current — he called this "retarded drag." Hence the following question.

DOES DAMP QUALIFY AS DRY?

One minor conundrum when discussing dry-fly methods is how to treat a floating fly which is intended to drag across the current either at the end of a dead drift or from the beginning of the cast. I pondered this question some time ago when reviewing *Salmon on a Dry Fly* (1987) by the British author Derek Knowles, whose ingenious fly designs are meant to be cast downstream and skimmed over the surface. The flies are tied with a deer hair skirt that makes them ride higher than a Buck Bug or Bomber when swinging across stream. Knowles came to Canada in 1987 in a sort of reverse LaBranche odyssey, unfortunately faring little better than the original traveler. Despite that, his small Yellow Dolly fly deserves a thorough trial.

Eventually, for no better reason than that it suits my purposes, I decided to include damp-fly techniques in this chapter.

TACTICS

Working a discovered fish or covering the water are both familiar tactics to the trout fisher and both have their place, albeit unequal, in salmon angling. Although I didn't see the first salmon I hooked on a dry fly, personal experience and conversations with many competent anglers have convinced me that fishing the dry fly blind over large waters is not overly productive. LaBranche's conclusion, supported by Hewitt, that large salmon will not move very far sideways for a dry fly seems to be justified. Hewitt even felt that you needed a good head of visible fish to be consistently successful, a situation rarely found today, particularly on public water.

For this reason I invariably begin with a wet fly unless a salmon is seen. Even in an unoccupied pool I would continue to try wet-fly tactics unless something showed. The exceptions are small pools or when there is a "special edge" along which a long dry-fly float is possible. Then I suggest using the dry/damp combination technique discussed below. Further, in a reversal from trout fishing experience, I believe more salmon are taken on downstream than upstream dead-drifts. Nonetheless, circumstances determine the approach, so several common situation will be treated individually.

IN COMPANY

Presume you are on public water and moving down the pool with the rest of the conga line. Perhaps you rise a salmon, or simply have a hunch, and decide to switch to a dry fly. As discussed later in Chapter 6, a reasonable leader tippet for salmon fishing tests eight pounds. This implies that flies in sizes six to ten match up well. Attach, say, a number 6 Bomber, rub in some floatant, and cast it across or across-and-down with lots of slack in the line and leader; should you have the water to yourself the fly can be cast up-and-across. The fly will drift downstream while you make as many mends as necessary, or possible, to prevent drag and prepare for the inevitable end of the float. Hopefully, the line will still be in position to skim the fly across stream at an attractive speed.

Now take two steps down — to make up for the extra time you took fishing the cast — but drop the fly three feet farther out. For round three add another three feet and then repeat the whole procedure. This provides better coverage than simply casting the same distance after each downstream advance.

The above is merely a dry-fly variation of the "greased line method" discussed in the last chapter. The fly floats dead-drift during the downstream portion of the cast and, depending on the pattern used, wakes in or sinks beneath the surface during the across-stream swing. If you want it to wake, use a Bomber or fat Buck Bug; if you want it to sink, use a slimly dressed (and ungreased) version of the latter. I specifically refer to deerhair flies in this situation because standard dry flies will swamp coming across stream. Although I have never tried them for salmon, Lee Wulff had considerable success with Skater type patterns in a variety of sizes and fished this way. When these high riders come across stream they hop and skip if the current is right or if the angler causes them to jump with hand or rod movements.

ON YOUR OWN

The sun, a high bank, and a careful approach just made you a finalist in the Lotto Salar draw. Lying down and peeking over the edge reveals a salmon (or several if you are friends with a leprechaun) resting beside a subsurface rock near the middle of the pool. Make sure you have the position well marked in your mind because when you get down to water level, that fish and the rock are probably going to be out of sight. Retreat slowly and enter the water cautiously below the quarry.

The reason I would try the upstream dry fly first? I believe you have a better chance to catch salmon in small clear pools if they can't see you. No, I can't prove it. My upstream successes might have been duplicated fishing down — who knows.

In any event, reduce the size of your tippet to 6 pounds and lengthen the leader to 10 or 12 feet, tie on a Wulff or small Bomber and start dead-drifting the fly over the fish. Just as in trout fishing, make the first cast to the near side of the salmon's position in case you have slightly misjudged the taking lane. Should a dozen casts return untouched, try a big (number 4) Bomber several times — an increase in tippet strength is required. In the larger sizes this fly is a mover and shaker but it's also notorious for being a better "raiser" than "hooker." Salmon seem to enjoy bumping a big Bomber with their noses, rolling on top of it, or slapping it with their tails. If you get some action, return to the smaller flies for awhile. Still no success? Now I would move above your frustration and give wet flies a try.

Another approach, suggested to me by Bill Ensor, is to stir up a sulky riser with motion. If a couple of dead-drifts are ignored,

Bill has had success by pulling a Bomber quickly over the head of the fish a few times and then offering it another dead-drift.

FROM A BOAT

Dry-fly fishing is often the preferred method from a boat, particularly in smooth water where the quarry can be seen. Downstream dead-drifts are the rule. Almost without exception, if you are in a boat, you will be in the hands of a guide and he will direct your casts.

ADDITIONAL OPPORTUNITIES

Although dry-fly fishing continues to gain recruits, there are still plenty of occasions where, on public water, other anglers will reel in at a point in the pool where the current speed is no longer sufficient to swim a wet fly properly. This presents an opportunity to work a dry fly in relative solitude over excellent holding areas, particularly when salmon locate themselves by rolling. You can also use the combination techniques by stripping to move the fly during the wet-fly swing.

Another opportunity, for the vigorous enthusiast, is a small river with long stretches of rocky runs between tiny pools. Take a lunch, an extra pair of socks, a pair of wading sneakers, a towel, and a pair of shorts in a pack along with a collapsible wading staff and start hiking. Shoot one or two casts to every likely looking pocket. Buck Bugs or small Bombers work best in these situations. Stay out of the water as much as possible, but when it's necessary to get in to cover a potential lie, wade wet in the sneakers and shorts. Naturally this is a warm weather activity.

Most suitable streams have very rocky shorelines, so wear a pair of good hiking boots and take the time to change when entering the water. Above all, be careful! Rocky bottoms can easily lead to the merely annoying scraped shin or the much more dangerous broken bone. Pocket hopping with a companion is a wise precaution. I know several experienced anglers who make a lot of entries on their catch record after these excursions.

STRIKING

The question of when to strike a skimming damp fly is easy enough to deal with because the line is tight and the salmon will hook itself. The primary concern will be to avoid taking the fly from the fish because you see it coming. Dead-drifting situations are more complex. On a long line, say fifty or sixty feet, striking immediately makes sense because by the time all the slack is taken out of the line and the impulse reaches the fly, the salmon probably has it. Closer in you must wait until the fish has turned down with the fly before tightening. It has been my experience with larger specimens of several species that while they are quick to reject an artificial dead-drifting subsurface, they are much more deliberate than small fish in taking dry flies.

AT THE END

It pays to carry a few sizes 12 and 14 trout flies in your box. Several times in the evening I've encountered salmon, in a couple of feet of water, rising steadily to a hatch of mayflies. I'd like to report that they succumbed to my expertise but that would be a lie. Failure is a poor professor, but at least you will have a shot with an appropriately sized imitation should this admittedly rare event occur.

There are also conditions of extremely warm water when only a very small dry fly will excite a rise. For reasons of conservation I oppose offering tiny flies to large salmon where they must be released. Unless you are very skilled, landing a large salmon on a size 18 hook and 5X tippet means you end up worrying it to death. Besides, salmon in water temperatures approaching 80 degrees are already highly stressed and a successful release becomes questionable.

In the previous chapter I mentioned Robert Pashley, whose magic touch was attributed to a condition that caused his hand to tremble continuously. A similar affliction can arise suddenly after a 20-pound fish, playing beaver, has just drowned your Bomber with a slap of its tail.

First Salmon — Dungarvon River, N.B. (Liz Wylie photo).

The crazy grilse pool — Nashwaak River, N.B.

Kelt

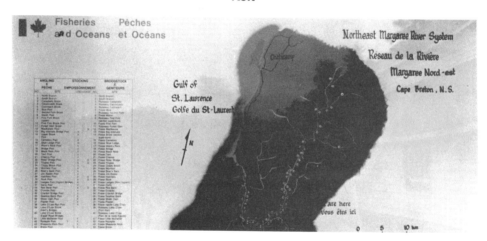

Pools — Margaree River, Nova Scotia

Bend Pool — Margaree River

Run — Margaree River

Part of bogan at bottom of Photo — MSW Miramichi River, N.B.

Ledge Pool — Margaree River

Plunge Pool (ASF photo)

Tidal pool at low tide — Better watch the canoe

Across and down (N.B. Tourism photo)

Staying Shallow

Bank — good for greased line — Margaree River

Downstream dry fly from a boat — Godbout River

CHAPTER 5

FISHING A POOL

INTRODUCTION

Having described pool types in Chapter 2 and the methods of presentation in the last two chapters, I think it's time to put the two together and fish. Like people, salmon pools can't all be treated the same way. While a few types discussed earlier ask little of the angler, others demand several changes in tactics as you work your way from head to tail. Although I cover all the ones mentioned earlier, the vast majority of my salmon have come from bend pools and runs. And I suspect it is the same for the majority of anglers. The bend pool is the most common, particularly on smaller rivers, and so there we'll start.

THE BEND POOL

(The diagram from Chapter 2 is repeated for convenience.)
A frequent angling mistake, and one easily avoided, is stomping out on the shingle for a look. If you're lucky or keen enough to be first rod of the day — remember someone has to be first, even on hard-fished public water — pretend you're trout fishing. Salmon do lie in shallow water or close to shore if undisturbed.

How shallow was made clear to me nearly twenty-five years ago. During my apprenticeship I often fished two popular public pools on the Main Southwest Miramichi River — Michael's Landing and Wasson's Bar. They were separated by a narrow bend pool where the current ran very swiftly over a gravel bottom. Because the gradient was fairly steep and constant, there was no slack water at the inside of the curve; instead a step had been carved out of the shingle — in effect, a six-inch miniature dropoff in eighteen inches of water.

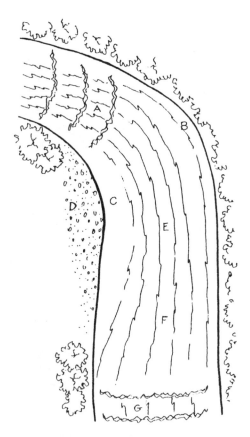

FIGURE 11. Figure 1 Repeated

On a day of plenty, fish and fishermen, my mentor Cliff Brown decided to move us from Michael's to Wasson's, which accommodates more anglers. On the way downriver he suggested I take a couple of casts in the fast run. I walked out to the edge of the shingle, cast, and then stepped out over the dropoff. As I did, I heard a typical chortling chide: "You're walking on the fish, Paul." I looked down, and sure enough a grilse powered his way upstream between my leg and the little underwater cliff.

Stepping hastily back onto dry land, I began casting so that the swing of the fly finished just at the edge of the dropoff. After a few casts I hooked and landed a grilse. It was a two-lesson episode. Lesson One was learned immediately: given the right cir-cumstances salmon will travel in very shallow water. To say ''lie'' wouldn't be accurate because these fish were most assuredly run-ning. And ''running'' was the subject of Lesson Two, which took further experiences to confirm. Many anglers argue that a running salmon won't take a fly. They are wrong. Settled salmon are a much better bet and I admit the anecdotal situation was unusual because it involved a very heavy run of fish, but I've taken moving salmon on other occasions over the years.

Sadly, the ice changed Michael's for the worse many years ago and it has yet to recover. However, what nature destroys she can also repair, a prime example being the swift stretch mentioned above. It's now a productive pool, although privately owned. One fine spring, with a little luck, some anchor ice will scoop out Michael's and it will again yield hundreds of salmon each year.

Just like a birddog with a nose for rabbits, I can't seem to stay on the scent of that bend pool we started fishing. At any rate, stay well back from the water and move carefully to the head (A on the diagram). Comb this area as thoroughly as your lover's hair. The current is swift and fish may not move far for the fly so I pull only a foot of line off the reel between each cast. In my experience if there's anyone home, the doorbell will often be answered. A point of courtesy occurs to me. You may arrive at a pool with high hopes of finding virgin water, only to discover that someone else has begun the seduction. Don't let disappointment ruin your manners. Don't wander up the shingle for a friendly chat. Make sure the cad is aware of your presence so he will start to move down, and then walk carefully upriver to await your turn.

After thoroughly fishing the head, keep lengthening the line until reaching the far shore or the limit of your casting range. Because of the fast water, try to keep the casts at a thirty-degree angle from the near bank. Before stripping in the line for the pick-up, let it rest straight downstream for a count of five — just in case of a follow. Now start taking a large stride after each cast.

Moving downriver the water gets deeper, the pool gets wider, casting gets harder. You become shorter, so to speak, so the back-cast has to be thrown higher to clear the stones behind. This may mean shortening the line. Listening carefully for any nasty little

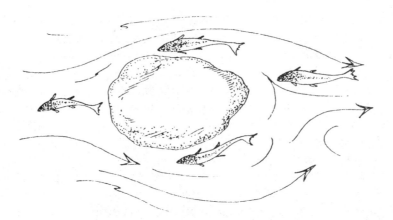

FIGURE 12. Possible Lies Around a Rock

ticks. Check the fly if you even dream you heard something and after every six throws just for safety. Don't wind up, just hand-line the fly in quickly to be sure it's got a point. Such trivial precautions would hardly be necessary if you were on the Godbout with Napoleon Comeau (a river guardian who got to fish when his millionaire friends were elsewhere) in 1874. On July 9th he landed 57 salmon between 8 and 24 pounds — the world's largest recorded single-day catch. But you're not there (unless you have mastered time travel), and that pull to a pointless hook may be the only offer you'll get.

Shortening the line may mean you can no longer reach the far bank with shallow-angle casts. This is not necessarily a disaster because the current may also be slowing down; casting more squarely across automatically picks up the speed of the fly. If you judge that the fly is fishing too quickly use the reach cast and mends to slow things down. Conversely, should you begin to feel like reciting ''The Charge of the Light Brigade'' between casts, stop leading the fly with the rod. Hold it perpendicularly to the bank to hurry up the swing. If more drastic action is required, begin to pull the fly slowly but smoothly with the line hand, or lead strongly with the rod.

Now I'd feel badly if I misled you into thinking that casting more across stream is always without peril. Sadly, many small rivers have naturally occurring Velcro just inshore from the shingle. As you square up the cast it enthusiastically attaches to your fly. There is no solution, save for learning a couple of casts which are better in these conditions than the overhead variety.

On occasion, you will find salmon sulking in the deepest part of the pool — and they will often be the big brutes. While it is tempting to spend plenty of time working these fish, they usually are extraordinarily reluctant. Depending on conditions (as always) it may be better to go looking for shallower lies where the salmon are often more co-operative.

After all this we come to the tail of the pool. The water gets shallower but the bush is now right at the bank, and the helpful shingle has disappeared. This area is deceptively attractive to salmon even during the brightest time of the day. Rocks providing comfortable lies stud the bottom and the current flows at a pleasant speed. But fishing this area properly poses a number of problems. Because the tail often widens quickly, it may take a long cast to cover. Unfortunately, at the point where you should begin to throw a longer line, you are still up to your thighs or higher in the central part of the pool. By the time your knees show above water you are too far into the tail to get coverage with shallow-angle casts. So the angler ends up casting square to the current just as the undergrowth makes its way to the water's edge.

A common reaction is to wade out into the tail but this may move salmon off their lies or at least unsettle them. Another catch is that as the line swings around it wants to carry the fly over the lip into the fast riffle below. I try to get around both these problems by adopting modified greased-line tactics (smoothly stripping line to keep it from going over the lip) combined with spey-style casts (described in a later chapter) which eliminate backcasts. Another excellent method, if the water isn't too deep, is to wade out *just* below the lip and cover the tail with an upstream dry fly.

THE RUN

The long run in a big river is a duffer's dream. Start at the top where everyone else gets in or even thirty feet upstream — sometimes there is a grilse hiding up there that others miss. Then

**Bogan from high up — main river split by island in foreground
and underwater edge of bar very visible (Olde River Lodge photo)**

Angler working plunge pool

lengthen the line and adjust the downstream angle until you can cover the same water as the rest of the world. The biggest strain is to keep one eye on your fly at all times in case a salmon rises; sometimes I drift away, entering the ''familiar road'' state — the eyes are alert for unusual events, but daydreams crowd out reality.

Where are you going to find fish in a run? Well, that depends largely on the number of salmon in residence. Guides and local anglers know which rocks or depressions are occupied first. You can often pinpoint these lies by watching (with the eye that isn't on the fly) the other fishermen. Do a few of them seem to pause and take more than one cast at a certain spot? Do they change the standard yard-long stride between casts for baby steps now and then? Where are people changing flies? (Only beginners give a yelp when they raise a fish.) Notice rock cradles where salmon have been kept after being caught — grilse are often landed near the point the angler was standing when he hooked the fish. Try listening to the experienced hands sitting on the bank waiting for their turn in the pool. (Even a polite question now and then will bring surprising results.) Finally, and perhaps most productively, ask your guide.

In a situation where there is a large run of fish, many uncommon lies will be occupied. A little beginner's luck will do because your fly will definitely cover fish. The most important step is to ensure that your fly is swinging in the same manner as that of the successful anglers. Don't be tempted to stretch for that extra ten feet at the expense of a controlled cast; keep your nerve and you will likely be rewarded.

Now suppose a salmon rises but misses (refuses) the fly. The gauntlet has been dropped. If fishing public waters with anglers behind you, local custom (which you took pains to learn) dictates your moves. Where I was brought up the rules were simple — one step backward and a couple of changes of fly were allowed. Take three or four minutes and then get moving again. If you are by yourself, my advice is to stay with this fish for a long time unless there is good reason to believe there are plenty of others around.

What's the plan? Opinions vary, but I believe in using a set-up pitch to offer the same fly. I always take one step backward, cast, and then repeat the cast from the position that brought the original rise. Unsuccessful? Try the pattern in the next smaller and then next larger size. *But never reel in to do this.* Still nothing? Only now start changing patterns in a preplanned sequence or in the disorder of desperation. Finally, adopt a series of different presentations with the original fly: a) vary the speed and angle of the fly's approach, b) put on a riffling hitch so that the fly leaves a wake, c) try a sinking braided leader to change the depth of presentation. After all that effort, rest the fish for awhile and then try a dry fly or a nymph. Of course, as in all things about angling, there is a school of thought that says stick with the original approach until bored. It rose the fish, didn't it?

Not every angler is emotionally prepared to undertake such protracted engagements. Long before all possibilities are exhausted you may decide that two birds in the bush are better than one in the hand. If so, take bearings on the spot you were standing when you got the rise and move on, intending to return later. A little pile of stones on the shore may make finding the hot spot easier. Salmon appear loathe to leave a lie until ready to continue migrating and will even return to it shortly after being disturbed.

Frequently these long runs end in a broad, deep, slow-moving pool. Here, even on otherwise crowded public water, you may discover as did Cowper, "How sweet, how passing sweet, is solitude!" The reason: most anglers, including myself, are intimidated by situations where you can only cover a small portion of the holding water and where the fly needs to be worked because of lack of current. Despite that, salmon are often seen in these pools, jumping and porpoising, as if preparing themselves for entering the run upstream. Frankly, I've had little success in these locations, due, I think, to a lack of confidence more than anything else. Len Wright, Jr., well known for his counter-current thoughts on fly-fishing, made a strong case for concentrating on deeper water and slower presentations in his book *Fly-Fishing Heresies* (1975). He recommended using a sink-tip to get down to where the big fish hang out in these pools.

BOGANS

As mentioned when I introduced you to bogans in Chapter 2, salmon will often lie in the slow water just where it meets the river's current. The best way to cover the mouth of a bogan is to cast the fly six feet or so into the slow water and mend the line quickly, perhaps several times, so that the fly enters the fast current as slowly as possible.

I've also referred before to the diagonal dropoff that begins at the upstream edge of many bogans. The position of this shallow lip may move around from year to year under the influence of the ice but you can always spot it by paying attention to the surface. There's a change in the ripple pattern just below the lip. Salmon, commonly grilse because the dropoff normally isn't very deep, like to take advantage of the subsurface eddy created.

Such a pool on the Main Southwest Miramichi has been a favorite of my brother and me for many years. Although I have taken several fish from the lip, Jim has done far better. Being the gentleman that he is he invariably suggests that I go through first. Too often I raise a salmon in that spot and then he, following behind, catches it. For some spooky reason several of the grilse he hooked in the pool have literally been walked immediately up the shingle like giant chub, a real disappointment.

Below bogans and other cold-water flows, including spring seepages, is another favorite lie of salmon in warm weather. The fish will often move in very close to shore, so taking care not to push them out is warranted. When the fly moves into areas like this at the end of a swing, don't be too anxious to pick it up. Let it work in this water for awhile. I always take a few extra casts around these spots and shorten my step. A little cold water brook exists into the main river from my brother's property and while he has been successful there a number of times, I can't remember it producing for me — timing I suppose. Another likely brook flows in just above the previously mentioned Michael's Landing, unfortunately on private property. I remember sneaking up there in my younger days to whip out a dozen sea trout on dry flies before the rest (or anyone else) got wise.

THE LEDGE POOL

Ledge pools are the bane of my existence. I know theoretically how to fish them depending on the circumstances but I can only

Morning on the Margaree

A Popular Spot on the St. Mary's

Advice on Fighting his First Salmon

Fall Color and High Water on the Dungarvon

A Gaggle of Bombers and Buck Bugs

Classic Green Highlander and the Hairwing Version

**A Modified Bomber tied by the inventor Rev. Elmer J. Smith
and a Spring Salmon Streamer**

**Wet flies discussed in the text — from left to right and top to bottom:
Rusty Rat; Cosseboom; Oriole; Black Bear, Green Butt;
Blue Charm; Marabou Muddler; Butterfly.**

remember being successful on one occasion. I waded far enough out above the ledge so that the fly finished each drift right at the edge of the ledge. The grilse took at the end of the swing where I expected. Others tell me that they have success bringing the fly slowly back toward them. A full sinking line or sink tip may work better because they keep the fly in the target zone; if you have the pool to yourself, an upstream nymph drifted along the edge of the ledge or pulling out the Patent may be the best bet.

If the ledge is on the far side of the river, at the base of a steep rock face, try casting right against the face at as shallow a downstream angle as possible. Then mend the line to keep the fly moving over the ledge slowly. Another possibility is to float a dry fly right above the edge of the dropoff. I've usually tried this tactic with a downstream dry because of other anglers in the pool. In the final analysis though, I don't like ledge pools and so avoid them.

PLUNGE POOLS

Plunge pools don't exist on the rivers I commonly visit. Where they are found, boats are often the only way to attack them because the banks are so steep on either side. The only time I ever did anything useful in one was on the Lahave River in Nova Scotia. I mentioned earlier my lack of success with the cruisers in the pool itself but I did manage a grilse right at the outlet where everyone congregates. This tail area is also a favorite haunt of the boat angler in pools which aren't accessible to wading anglers. The smooth surface flows are perfect for dry-fly work.

Trying to take a salmon from a side eddy in a plunge pool can also be an interesting experience. I've seen anglers manage the feat by using variations of the Patent. They cast (a short cast) a big fly out to the edge of the main stream and then let it carry the fly into the eddy and back towards them. The fly sank down several feet and the salmon rose to take it — definitely a close encounter because you must be able to see the fish rise and strike quickly. Actually, this whole exercise is a bit academic because plunge pools aren't abundant in the more accessible rivers.

STILLWATERS

By now it should be clear that I prefer pressure on my waders. Lakes, ponds, and deadwaters leave me unmoved. To fish for salmon in lakes you can troll or cast in front of visible cruisers. As far as ponds and deadwaters go, I've caught the grand total of one salmon in three or four attempts. That was in the Salmon Hole on Nova Scotia's Moser River and it came to a Black Bear, size 12 double, cast out and allowed to sink before being twitched back. Hardly a world of experience to pass on.

In the section on plunge pools I suggested fishing the outlet. The same goes for ponds, which also have the added attraction of an inlet. One technique I've seen succeed at an inlet is to cast a dry fly on a short line and let the current carry the fly as far out into the pond as possible while you feed slack line through the guides.

NON-POOL POOLS

In Chapter 4 I mentioned the pack-and-rod approach to the long stretches of broken water often found in the headwaters of salmon rivers. But you don't have to be a great tramper to take advantage of these opportunities. On many rivers the majority of fishermen prefer to drive between the pools even when separated by a mile or less. Taking to the river bank may not score often but solitude and the occasional salmon scooped out of a lie you discovered yourself might be reward enough.

A FEW NOTES ON SMALL POOLS

Small pools are at once both the easiest and hardest to fish — easiest because covering every inch of water is possible, hardest because they often require the most sensitive line handling. Small pools and rocks are frequent companions. The latter are often large enough to affect the swing of the fly, so line control is critical. It's also in places like this that I believe concealment is of the utmost importance. My tactic is to treat them like trout pools and conceal myself and my casting as much as possible.

I repeat that salmon seldom reveal their awareness of humans. But aware they are and it may disturb them. For example, on a beautiful Monday in July, we were fishng a pool in the middle reaches of the Little Southwest Miramichi. It is a popular spot and quite clearly had been hammered during the weekend. Our cautious approach to several fish visible from the high bank came to naught. They were skittish and even moved off their lies occasionally when our flies swung in front of their noses or overhead.

At one point a good fish rolled and then jumped on the far side of the river. I waded out for a try, unsuccessfully, and then sat down on a midstream rock to think. Looking down into the water I discovered I had a companion. A grilse had taken up residence on the far side of the rock. Every so often he would move several inches ahead until he could see me face to face but he made no attempt to abandon ship. Even when I dribbled a dozen flies in front of his nose he simply ignored me.

With the foregoing in mind, try to cover the whole of a small pool from one spot. To begin, if I don't see any fish, I favor a downstream dry (almost exclusively a Buck Bug) floated along the current lanes and pulled under at the end of the drift to swing into my shore. Don't lift right away for the next cast but pull the fly back several feet. Extend the float by shaking out additional line pulled from the reel. If this is unsuccessful tie on a wet fly and cover the ground again, being careful to control the speed of the fly by mends, rod position or motion, or pulling in line where necessary. Although the swings will be short, if you don't pay attention the current tongues will push the fly line into contortions.

CONCLUSION

When approaching a pool you have all the tactics discussed in previous chapters at your disposal. Many times company will force a choice upon you, although you still have the option of what type of line to use. Try to visualize what the bottom looks like and adjust accordingly. When you have the luxury of solitude, select a method which appears to give the most attractive coverage of the water and be stealthy.

CHAPTER 6

TACKLE

RODS

Although perhaps an unorthodox way to introduce the essentially technical subject of tackle, the following anecdote reveals both the capabilities of light gear and the advantage of being blessed with angling luck. The story was told to me by Jack Eschenmann, a fine trout and salmon angler from the talent-rich Cumberland Valley area of Pennsylvania.

In the late 1970's or 1980 a friend and I decided to drive around the Gaspe Peninsula. Our purpose was sightseeing, not fishing. We drove up the Matapedia and down the Matane and then along the North Shore past all those beautiful rivers. Arriving at the towers of Gaspe we decided to rest up a couple of days. So I asked my friend if she would mind if I did a little fishing. There being no objections, the next day I bought a fishing license and a permit to fish the Dartmouth. After getting directions I drove upstream some 15 to 20 miles and pulled over at a well used parking area.

True to original intentions I had no salmon gear but my trout rod, trout flies and hipboots are as much of a fixture in the trunk as the spare tire. The 6½ foot Shakespeare glass fly rod and "large" #12 dry flies along with a couple of streamer flies seemed about right for a pleasant day of casting practice.

About that time a local angler pulled in and got ready to fish. We soon found out that communication was limited as he spoke little English and I could only understand basic French if spoken slowly. In any event, while looking with considerable amusement at my outfit, he told me that yesterday his brother had taken a 20 and a 25 lb. salmon from this pool. After offering one of his double hooked flies, size 1/0, he told me where

the salmon lies were and asked me to fish through first. I insisted I'd follow him down. After covering 50–60 yards of the
pool he motioned for me to get in at the top. Once in position
I now had the problem of casting that 1/0 meathook with a 5
wt. line on a 6½ ft. rod. After almost hitting myself in the back
of the head with the fly I finally got it about where I wanted.
Of course it plunged to the bottom like a lead sinker.

After my third cast I thought the fly had hung up on a
weed so I gave a strong jerk on the rod. To my amazement
the largest Atlantic salmon I've ever seen came up, jumped
and took off downstream. Fortunately, I always put about 100
yds of Cortland 15 lb. test backing on all my fly reels. The
salmon ran about 75 yards downstream and stopped. Instead
of going after him I tried a method I've used successfully on
large Chinook salmon. By immediately stripping out about
15–20 feet of line and letting the fairly strong current carry it
below the salmon, the pull began to come from downstream.
He slowly swam back to the spot where he'd first felt the hook.
I was glad to retrieve my line but the relief was short lived.
As soon as I had a tight line, on went the pressure. Again he
came completely out of the water but this time he went
upstream about 75 yards. The fight continued in this position
and it was one of the most intense tussles I've experienced.
Finally, with both angler and quarry severely weakened, my
companion slipped an experienced hand around the salmon's
"wrist" and tailed him. The battle had lasted 45 minutes. The
scale I use for weighing Chinooks pulled down to 32 pounds
— my largest Atlantic salmon.

My helpful partner in this triumph indicated he would like
to have the fish if I intended to release it and I happily obliged.
I'd hoped to keep the fly as a memento of this wonderful day;
however, the gentleman wanted the fly back and as his fly box
was not very well stocked I returned it with many thanks.

Jack's story is more than just a record of victory with a short
rod (Lee Wulff championed them for decades). It's also a graphic
illustration of how good technique can shift the odds in favor of
the angler. In any event, I didn't include this anecdote as an en-
dorsement of tiny trout rods any more than I'd send you out to

buy a double-handed fifteen footer, the size favored by so many British salmon anglers. But if you are off on a first foray for Atlantics it demonstrates that there's no need for special gear. A seven or eight-weight bass or heavy trout stick will do the job.

At one time I used ten-foot rods strung with a 10 or 11-weight line, believing that I needed power and weight to handle wind. Lately, however, I have switched to 9½ foot, 8-weights that are quite capable of dealing with all but the worst conditions. A useful feature of many heavier line weight rods is a "fighting butt." This permanent or removable piece extends beyond the reel seat and permits the angler to put the rod butt into his midriff while keeping the reel clear.

Nonetheless, it must be said that British salmon anglers know a thing or two about this game. A long rod will increase your casting range as you wade above the buns. It also makes a number of the line repositioning methods discussed earlier far more efficient. Recently I've experimented with two-handed rods made by Sage and Loomis. Learning to cast without help was a painful and only marginally successful effort. The potential is so obvious, however, that I intend to persevere.

Being of average means, my path led from glass to graphite and only rarely have I handled bamboo. Frankly, I didn't enjoy the experience, probably because the vastly different action threw me off completely. Should you plan to invest in a new rod, let me make one suggestion — never buy one you haven't tried. Find some way to cast several different makes in the line weight of your choice, perhaps through a club if a good store with a casting pond isn't available.

While it seems rather obvious, take care of your rod. Salmon fishing often involves traveling between a number of pools during a day and it's tempting to break the rod down, wind up the line to hold the two pieces together, and then stick it in the trunk or back of the truck to avoid taking the time to restring it at each stop. I'm guilty of this crime from time to time and undeservedly have escaped paying the penalty. Beyond the chance to break or weaken the rod by a nick (quite devastating with some of the latest graphites), it's hard on the guides and the inevitable dust does the reel no good. Each time you prepare to move, put everything away in its appropriate case.

**Reels photo — Top row from left to right:
Cortland 140 Magnum, J W Young 1530;
Center row from left to right: Hardy Princess 3½,
Hardy Marquis Salmon No. 1; Bottom row: Bryson Salar**

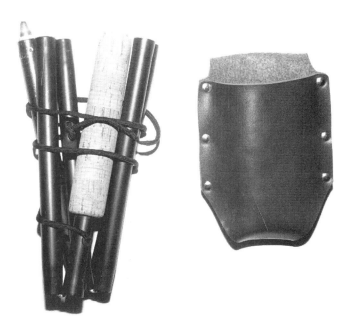

Wading staff

REELS

Some adjustment to your reels may be required. As Jack's story emphasizes, you need lots of backing should a little pixie dust rub off on your fly or in the challenging circumstances of a lively fish under difficult conditions. Take your largest trout reel and get as much twenty-pound test Micron backing on the spool as possible. If you can't wind on at least 100 yards — 150 yards is preferable — then consider buying a new reel. There are a number of good models in the fifty-dollar bracket, not fancy but well constructed.

Reels are designated either single-action or multiplying. The former are equipped with a fixed or adjustable drag. Contrary to popular belief there is no need to have an adjustable drag. My first salmon reel was a J.W. Young, having only a fixed click drag sufficient to prevent overrunning before my brain caught up with the reality of a take. It landed plenty of salmon. The brand has become available again after disappearing for many years from the North American market but the design has changed (including the addition of an adjustable click) and I have no experience with the newer versions. By the way, I absolutely abhor reels with lots of screws in the assembly because the screws tend to fall out at the most inconvenient times.

For reasons more acquisitive than technical, I presently use single-action reels with adjustable click or clutch drags. The latter are excellent for exerting a heavy uniform resistance and reducing the time to bring a salmon to hand. On the downside, smooth as they may be, they can never be as sensitive as your hand, and a fish that suddenly starts jerking can cause a nasty parting of the ways. Also, if you tighten the drag during a fight and then forget to loosen it again before the next take . . . #@#! And anyhow, the wail of a tortured click is a sound I have no intention of forgetting.

Multiplying reels operate on the same principle as spinning reels and provide more than a single turn of the spool for each revolution of the handle. In addition they are anti-reverse, meaning that the spool will turn against the drag while the handle is held fixed. The advantages of fast line take-up are obvious as is the protection against scraped knuckles. Two drawbacks are the aforementioned possibility of setting the drag too tightly and their high cost.

LINES

Much of the salmon fishing in North America occurs during the warm-weather season when a floating line is all that is needed. Assuming you already do some trout fishing, you probably have a weight-forward line in your kit and it would be a rare event to find any other style on the river. One could fish successfully with a double-taper line, but when trying to cover water most people find the weight-forward easier to use. While there are plenty of brands available, far more than there are actual manufacturers, I've never been disappointed by the quality of Cortland or Scientific Angler products.

Recently I've fished with a Lee Wulff Triangle Taper, which, while adding ten feet to my maximum cast and eliminating sagging loops when stretching for distance, requires excessive false casting to work the taper beyond the guides. Because the taper is forty feet long — and you need to leave this length beyond the tip for smooth casting — the pick-up can be a little difficult for less experienced casters. I guess you can't have everything.

To be fully equipped, you might find it helpful to have a sink-tip and an intermediate line available on spare spools. I recommend a Cortland Type IV/fast-sinking tip if you need to get down in a hurry. The intermediate line is a help in getting a recalcitrant fly to sink or when cold water suppresses the salmon's willingness to come all the way to the surface to take. There is, however, a price to be paid when using intermediate lines which I mentioned in an earlier chapter. Consequently, I don't use them, preferring instead to switch to sinking leaders.

As for line color, dark below the surface, light on top seems to be the standard. Over the years no one has produced evidence, although there's plenty of speculation, that, for example, white is better than yellow.

LEADERS

During nearly a quarter century of salmon angling, while I've had my share of misadventures, I can remember only one instance of breaking a leader. Fortunately, salmon aren't particularly leader-shy except in very low, clear conditions, so there is normally no need to chance lossess on gossamer tippets in an expectation of more hook-ups.

The simplest style of leader is a uniform piece of monofilament the length of the rod; it's popular with many salmon anglers. Eight or 10-pound test is a good choice, depending on the size of fly and size of fish you expect to catch. A short piece of 20-pound mono is nail-knotted to the line and a loop is formed at the other end. The main leader is attached to this butt piece with a loop-to-loop connection. Another method is the braided butt section discussed below. Although there are several high quality brands of monofilament available, Maxima seems to be the runaway favorite on the rivers I've fished during the last fifteen years.

While opting for simplicity from time to time, my desire for ever-longer casts dictates getting all the help possible to turn the fly over. Consequently, I use 9 or 10-foot knotless tapered leaders testing 8 or 10 pounds at the tip. My choice in recent years is tapers designed by Dave Whitlock and sold by Umpqua Feather Merchants.

One relatively recent innovation is the braided leader. These are available in floating, intermediate, and a variety of sink rates (see Table 1). The Chinese finger-puzzle type of attachment to the line means that it's easy to change leaders. The upshot is that you can convert a floating line to a short sink tip by the addition of the appropriate sink-rate leader. The manufacturers recommend a double surgeon's knot to attach a length of mono to the thin end of the leader. I usually add about three feet to the end of the braided sinking leaders.

Because I prefer to use monofilament leaders most of the time (although I intend to experiment extensively with intermediate braided leaders), I've installed braided butts, available from Orvis, on all my lines. These are three-inch braided monofilament with a loop at one end. By forming a loop at the large end of the sinking braided leaders, I can switch back and forth to my heart's content. (See Figure 13 for details.) I tried putting a loop in the thin end as well so that I could replace the mono tippet without knots but the loops didn't stand up (discovered while trout fishing, thankfully!)

TABLE 1. BRAIDED LEADERS

AIRFLO LEADERS

SECONDS PER FOOT	INCHES PER SECOND	SECONDS PER METRE	
			& Monofilament Leader
—	—	—	Floating LSR 0
23.5	0.5	80	Intermediate LSR 1
13.2	0.9	45	Antiwake LSR 2
4.4	2.6	15	Slow Sinking LSR 4
2.9	3.9	10	Fast Sinking LSR 8
2.1	5.6	7	Super Fast Sinking LSR 16
0.9	13.1	3	Extra Super Fast Sinking LSR 24

When I want the fly to fish well below the surface I still use a fast-sinking sink-tip line but I usually add a braided sinking leader as well. This gives me a longer sinking tip that's tapered to a thinner point. You might find the braided leaders an attractive and inexpensive alternative to carrying spare spools.

FIGURE 13. Making Loop In Butt of Braided Leader

KNOTS

As I said in the introduction, this book is not intended to teach you all about fly-fishing. On the other hand, salmon anglers commonly use a knot with which you may not be familiar. It's the Turle Knot and it can be used with turned-up or turned-down eyed hooks. It is quite strong, being rated at around 90 percent of the leader strength. I've never had one break. I have, however, had the higher-rated clinch knot come undone several times, leaving that ugly little pigtail (my fault I know). Despite that, there are ring-eyed streamer patterns that require a clinch knot. The Turle Knot earns its way because the leader passes through the eye with the knot itself set behind the eye. This prevents the knot from sliding around the eye, which can ruin the swim of the fly. Instructions for tying the Turle are given in Figure 14. I suggest you practice it a hundred times until you can tie it with your eyes closed.

I don't particularly like knots in my leader. Aided by the convenience of the braided butt, if conditions demand a longer, finer leader, I change the whole leader. When the tippet section of a

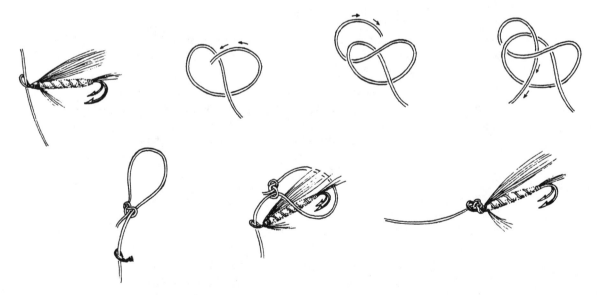

FIGURE 14. Turle Knot Sequence

tapered mono leader has been cut back a couple of feet, I replace the whole thing. Who wants to lose a large salmon for the sake of a buck and a half?

WADERS

Unless you are going to do all your salmon fishing from a boat, you'll need waders. And hip boots won't suffice. There are just too many situations where you have to get into waist-deep water. I'm a big booster of Neoprene. These days it doesn't cost much more than rubberized fabric and you'll actually win the odd battle with streamside bushes — although barbed wire is still boss. Other advantages are ease of walking and extra warmth during fall fishing. The downside is that all that insulation is the last thing needed in the summer. Rolling them down to your waist will bring some relief but if it's 80 degrees you're still going to sweat a bunch. One little hint for surviving hot weather is to carry a few drinks in the back of your vest to avoid dehydration headaches.

Neoprene is available in both boot-foot and stocking-foot models. The stocking-foot type provides greater flexibility and can be turned inside out to dry. I always travel with pairs of lightweight hip and chest stocking-foot waders as well and so one pair of wading boots serves all. The advantage of the boot-foot style is that you'll win all the races to the pool and be first to escape to the vehicle when the mosquitoes have scented blood. Regardless of which type you choose make sure that the bottom of the boot has a felt sole. While some rivers have a pleasant bottom of sand or gravel, others feature nature's equivalent of oversized greasy ball bearings. Fortunately, the wading is rarely difficult enough to require hob nails or cleats.

WADING STAFFS

I'll never forget working down a pool on the Renous River, and in my desire for one last cast, getting into a position where the current was too heavy to go back or turn around. My brother had to get a branch, wade out until we could lock arms and then work our way slowly back to shore. A wading staff would have solved my problem.

There are many styles of staff on the market but I strongly recommend the fold-up type. It fits in a leather pouch strapped to your waist until you need it and then with a shake it extends. Oh, I've used everything from a discarded ski pole to a tree limb, but the latter is a scary and unreliable tool and the former is a nuisance when not needed. Since a staff can save you from a ducking or worse it makes sense to have the best and most convenient type. If it's not convenient you'll be tempted to leave it back at camp.

ODDS AND SODS

Most of the oldtimers I used to fish with on the Miramichi never used a vest. One box of flies and a spool of tippet material was all they carried. This minimal kit fit nicely into the pocket in the inside top of their waders. On the other hand, there are people like me who wouldn't be without the following:

1. Rainjacket
2. At least four boxes of flies
3. Several spools of tippet material
4. Spare tapered leaders
5. Flashlight
6. Hook hone
7. Haemostats
8. Polaroids
9. Spare reel spool
10. Insect repellent
11. Clippers
12. Fly floatant
13. Leader sink
14. Nymph indicators

I definitely need a vest, one with lots of pockets. The choice is yours.

Although hardly a matter of great concern to the modern angler, the choice of container for carrying flies was once of great cultural significance. While I have no direct evidence concerning the origin of the word "flybook," I recently ran across the following possibility. In *The Practice of Angling* (1855), O'Gorman suggests, "Tear, then, as many leaves out of any novel which you may find, on perusal, worthless, or abounding with immoral descriptions, and fill their places with parchment covers, open at one end, and the full height and the sides of the binding of the volume — by these means, your flies can be made up tolerably large, full as large as the breadth of the book — then for colours, you need only sew some leather ends to prevent them from flying out, in any of those works that may be of little or no value as food for the mind." O'Gorman gives a list of authors whose works he would have you spare, but *The Monastery* by Scott and Byron's *Ode to Napoleon* are recommended for flies.

Regardless of what you may read or see elsewhere, almost no one carries a tailer to land fish. And while you have little choice when alone, handtailing is difficult for beginners. If you are going to release your catch, then it's conservation-minded to land the salmon as soon as possible. A good man on the net and a cool angler can cut many minutes off the fight. I honestly believe this is more important than the few scales lost during netting — which can be minimized by using a net with a cotton, knotless mesh. If you plan to kill the fish, then once again the net is the safest way. When two or more walk to the river, one should be carrying a big net.

A FINAL WORD

If you take only one bit of the advice I offer, other than the lifesaving qualities of a good staff, then let it be the following. Salmon, particularly large specimens, are few and far between. To lose one due to carelessness, regardless of its ultimate disposition, is both disheartening and shows a lack of respect for the quarry. It's like hunting with a poorly sighted rifle. Although I've encountered this counsel in many different forms, none said it better than Capt. J. Hughes-Parry, an outstanding Welsh salmon angler, in his book *A Salmon Fisher's Notebook*.

Granted some of what he says is a little outdated (for example we no longer have to soak our casts, although you could easily substitute checking for wind knots or abrasions), but you'll get the point. To wit, ''An angler's behaviour towards his different tools tells its own story. A line which has not been run off the reel for its whole length and then carefully rewound, at least at the beginning of the season; a cast which has not been soaked overnight and then tested link by link — these are only two examples of man's ill-conduct towards his servants, and by these lapses he, and not they, is weighted in the balance by the Lesser Gods and found wanting. I have said before that hooks should be kept needle-sharp, and that some men will even go so far as to miss a ring when threading their line and never trouble to put it right. Are they going the right way to work? Too much care cannot be taken in even the very minutest details, for on them so much of success depends.''

Just in case you don't believe the importance of all these little details, witness the unfortunate Major W.G. Greenaway. Telling his story in ''Easy Lessons In The Angling Art,'' reprinted in *The Atlantic Salmon Treasury* (1975), he laments the loss of a salmon due to a failure to rewind the reel backing, which at a critical moment jammed and promptly snapped. Normally this would not be a tragedy, but in his case the salmon was gaffed (poached?) two days later with the fly still in its jaw. It weighed 74 pounds!

CHAPTER 7

CASTING

Although the ability to cast well is important in all branches of fly-fishing, it is imperative on a salmon river — not only for the obvious reason of being able to cover the lies. In a week of angling you may conceivably make fifteen thousand casts. With outrageous good fortune you could expect to succeed with twenty-eight of these. If even one tenth of the rest are bungled, you will quickly become frustrated and depressed. It's not at all like trout fishing, where time is spent moving into position, with relatively few casts made to the same spot. On a big salmon river you might be called on to stretch to your limit time after time.

Temptation is a terrible thing. I've reviewed many books over the years and have steadfastly maintained that casting cannot be taught well on the printed page. On the other hand, in an introductory text, there seems to be a void if casting is omitted. I intend to stick by my principles and resist. If you have never cast a fly and intend to go salmon fishing, then try to get an experienced flyfisher to instruct you, or invest in a casting school. The next best thing is to acquire one of the several good fly-casting videotapes.

The rest of this chapter assumes you have some fly-casting skills and concentrates on a number of special problems that arise in salmon fishing. The first of these is related to wading. To get an immediate feel for the effects of wading, go out on open land and make a few casts from your knees. That makes keeping the backcast up difficult, doesn't it? Rivers invariably have banks, without which they would be swamps. Even the most benign background, a smoothly sloping shingle, still rises several feet above the water level. Most people don't realize that casting distance is related to how far the line is above the ground or water during the strokes (the reason tournament casters work from platforms).

For example, when standing on the ground and using a nine-foot rod the line is about fourteen feet up unless you are adept at

Lefty Kreh's high backcast techniques. When you wade into the river up to your waist you have lost three feet of height. In addition to this the stroke for the backcast has been reduced. Both these factors combine to shorten the length of line you can throw.

As mentioned previously, the head of the pool is usually the narrowest and shallowest part. So you start out in the best possible position, up to your ankles and needing the shortest line. As you move into the pool the water often deepens and the river widens. You naturally reach out to try and cover all the water, but as you call for more line the available height for the backcast diminishes. All this is simply to say that you should not be discouraged; it's a fact of life that you will run out of range more quickly than expected.

The second factor which reduces casting range is what I call the turn. Those of you familiar with books or videos or casting schools will know that virtually no one ever mentions the turn. Here's what I mean: An ordinary down-and-across cast finishes with the line straight below you. The goal is to pick up the line and send it out at a 45- (more or less) degree angle down-and-across again. To do this you must change the direction of the line. One way to do this is to false-cast several times until the entire plane of the cast is in the direction you want to throw. Now the line will go out straight. However, this means a lot of extra casts and may subject you to the bushes that grow three feet taller and creep three feet closer to the river as soon as you turn your back on them.

If you attempt to pick up the line into a backcast that travels straight upriver and then redirect the forward stroke down-and-across by a curved motion of the arm, the end of the line with the leader has a tendency to curl upriver — not a desirable result. One way to avoid this is to move the rod smoothly upstream until it points in the direction you want the forward cast to go and then, without stopping, begin the pick up. This is not a cure-all because turning the line on the backcast sucks some of your available power and thus reduces the amount of line you can pick up. Another bit of nastiness is that the bushes are still there. You should experiment with some intermediate positions which might be more comfortable and yield only a small amount of curvature at the end of the forward cast.

(A to D) Spey cast sequence

The second problem I'll deal with is more difficult to resolve. In fact I'm going to have to break the rule I set only a few paragraphs ago and try and teach a cast because you won't learn it anywhere else. Right-handed anglers abhor the situation depicted in Figure 15 (left-handers should reverse sides of the river). This diagram is a fairly accurate representation of Big McDaniel pool on the Margaree River. A few years ago I watched several anglers trying to fish this pool with standard casting techniques and their flies seemed to spend more time in the bushes than in the water. Others were getting out a line without hanging up but the right-handers were not getting a good coverage of the run because a short line was all they could manage. In fact, I know folks who simply won't fish pools that look like this. The turn required to get out a good straight line is severe and robs the cast of much of its power. The only way to overcome this as far as I'm concerned is to learn a Spey cast.

Spey casting is associated with two-handed rods, still widely used in Britain and Norway. However, it is possible with a little practice and determination to learn how to make Spey casts with a single-handed rod. For the single Spey, first face the direction

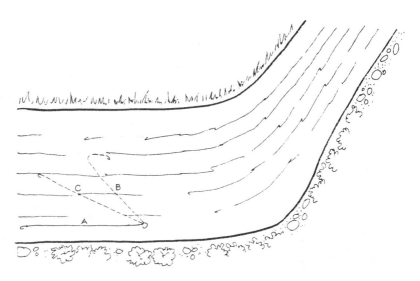

FIGURE 15. Problem of casting from left side

in which you want the cast to go (although contrary to most instruction, I do better with my left foot forward). Next, with the rod pointing straight downstream and parallel to the water, lift it slowly into the air. This starts the line toward you. Keep your line hand close to your rod hand. Now swing the point of the rod down and upstream in a U motion, still keeping the line hand close to the rod hand. This motion will move the line upstream of your position. Keep the rod moving into a roll-cast position and rock your body rearward. At the instant the line touches the water, go into a roll-cast delivery, rocking your body forward while at the same time hauling down with the line hand. Aim the roll cast upward and release the line in the left hand, allowing extra line to shoot out (see photo sequence pages 72–73).

Mike and Denise Maxwell of Gold-N-West Flyfishers, Vancouver, are widely acknowledged experts in Spey casting, and Mike tells me that Denise can punch out the whole fly line with a single-handed rod. My best efforts are sixty-five or seventy feet. With a two-handed rod, competent casters can easily get into the backing.

What I described above is not easy to learn. In fact if you read British texts they will almost uniformly state (even though they all try to teach it) that Spey casting can only be learned from an instructor. Unfortunately, it's virtually impossible to find such an instructor in eastern North America. If you get the chance to visit the west coast, look up Mike and Denise Maxwell, or another fanatic steelheader — likely to be a capable performer. The toughest part is to judge the amount of force necessary to move the line upstream far enough to get it all upstream of the caster but not throw it into an aerial backcast. Only practice solves this problem.

A drawback to the single Spey is that if you encounter a strong downstream wind it tends to blow the line into the angler. The solution is the double Spey, but I find this difficult to execute with a single-handed rod (particularly off the left shoulder). The Maxwells point to my favorite fast graphite rods as the biggest handicap. Should you decide to give it a try, refer to the series of photos in which Denise Maxwell makes it look easy. The rod is a 9-foot 6-inch Gold-N-West, Tigereye II, 8-weight. Mike recommends the Scientific Angler Steelhead Taper floating line. What follows is Mike's description of the action:

Double Spey (Mike Maxwell photos)

1. Line downstream to the right — rod pointed downstream. Right foot forward in cast direction — body leaned forward — rod tip dipped down to water to produce the maximum line tension when lifted.

2. Body still leaned forward — rod lifted. Starts line moving — tensions the line — bends the rod — allows caster to judge the power required for the upstream sidecast.

3. Body leaned forward — upstream sidecast to the left places a loop above the water to the left — the end of the line and the fly anchored in the water downstream to the right ready for the circular rockback backcast.

4. The body rocked back — as the rod and line are swung around to the right rear. The end of the line and fly anchored in the water downstream to the right ready for the forward rock, power forward cast.

5. The body rocked forward — rod pushed upwards and outwards. The line well above the water — just like a good overhead forward cast — not down on the water like a rollcast.

6. The line still above the water and almost extended. The rod tip is being lowered at the same speed as the line falls.

7. The line is on the water and straight out in the direction that the caster pushed it during the forward cast. The rod tip is dipped down to the water ready for immediate action.

Although many anglers don't realize it, a weight-forward line has a lot in common with a shooting head. A shooting head won't function if you have more than a foot or so of the running line outside the tip guide on the pick-up. A weight-forward line is a little more forgiving but it still operates best (without false casting) if only the first thirty to thirty-five feet of line is outside the tip. If the leader is ten feet long this means that to make a seventy foot throw in one pick-up and cast, you must shoot thirty feet of line.

What are you to do with this shooting line? As you bring in the line after the swing, it must be dropped on the water or coiled in loops. A normal strip pulls in about three feet, so this means about ten pulls. This much line on the water will definitely impede the shoot. Conversely, ten loops held in the hand are ripe for a tangle on their way through the guides. One answer is a shooting basket, although they are rarely seen on a salmon river. Despite that, I have recently acquired one and intend to give it a try. What I do now is to drop the first five pulls on the water and then loosely drape the next five or so over my line hand, keeping each loop separated. This isn't 100 percent foolproof, but it works for me when using floating lines. Another trick is to hold the loops lightly in your lips. I've used this technique to good advantage when wading deep, but you must be very confident of the water quality before doing this all day.

One thing is certain: if you are not an expert, your casting will let you down at some point during a five-day trip. There are very few trout fishers who have any experience with constant casting for this length of time. You will show the effects of fatigue. When it happens, shorten up for a while to get your timing back. Check to see if you are hurrying the cast or starting the backcast with the rod held too high. Above all, don't get discouraged — it happens to everyone.

CHAPTER 8

FLIES

INTRODUCTION

Back in Chapter 1, I argued that salmon don't feed in fresh water but do "take" food. Some claim that if this is true, then a salmon in a good mood will grab any pattern in front of its nose that's properly presented. Alas, or perhaps thankfully, this isn't true. If my belief in remnant-feeding memory is sound, then it's anybody's guess which fly characteristics will trigger a reaction. With little in the way of guidance, such as the imitation of natural insects in the case of trout flies, thousands of patterns have been developed over the centuries. Most have faded into obscurity except to adorn pattern books, museum displays, or exhibition boxes, but a few continue to earn their keep in company with the hot flashes that seem to appear every year. However, before discussing patterns, let's take a quick look at hooks.

HOOKS

Customarily, modern salmon flies in North America are tied on special hooks. The standard wet fly version is made of heavy wire (2X stout, where 2X represents twice the value of a standard trout hook) with a black finish and has a turned-up, loop eye. Available in single and double-hook designs and in sizes 4/0 to 10, they have a shank length slightly longer than an equivalent trout hook.

There is the usual inconsistency when dealing with the products of different manufacturers; one man's #4 may have many characteristics of another's #6. Another difference between the two major manufacturers, Partridge and Mustad, is that the Partridge hooks have a tapered loop eye while the Mustad equivalents are made with an oval loop eye. The former is descriptive and in the latter the wire at the end of the loop has a blunt end. I prefer Partridge hooks but there is a cost differential (Table 2 illustrates various styles of Partridge salmon hooks).

Both Partridge and Mustad offer a low-water hook which is lighter and slightly longer than an equivalent "standard" size. The term low-water, when applied to fly dressing, signifies a pattern tied on the front two-thirds (or less) of the hook. This yields a small fly in terms of dressing while retaining the strength and gape of a larger hook. Frankly, other than the possibility of hooking "short strikers," I never understood why such flies were not tied on a short shank hook (same gape and wire size) instead of one longer than the "standard" size.

Another popular hook available from Partridge is the Wilson Dry Fly. It's 2X fine but 6X long and ends up weighing more than a standard hook with the same gape. Regardless of the name it is only rarely used for dry flies. Instead it is associated with low-water dressings, particularly those originally tied by A.H.E. Wood. Many of the dry/damp flies in use today are tied on standard wet-fly trout hooks. Most of the professional tiers I know use a Mustad 3908.

Arguments over whether single or double hooks are best have simmered for over a century. In my experience it doesn't make much difference which you use for hooking and holding salmon. I have many patterns in both styles and favor doubles in faster water because when slimly dressed they will sink a bit farther with less tendency to roll on their side. I'd recommend that you carry at least a few doubles.

GENERALITIES

While not particularly instructive as far as the individual pattern is concerned, it's worth noting that a wild departure from the tactic, "in X river at Y water level and Z temperature use Q" can occasionally be effective. Too many years ago I was working Big Pool on the Renous River along with seven or eight other anglers. The July sun was droughty and the river low and clear. The water

had endured a severe thrashing since daybreak and by early afternoon most of us were part of the second wave.

After several passes through the pool with no result I was feeling decidedly rebellious. Everyone was using floating lines and
small flies so I switched to a sink-tip line and knotted on a size
2/0 Alexandra (silver body, peacock herl wing), the largest fly I had
in my box. Betting that any salmon would be hiding from the sun
in the fast water at the head of the pool, I started higher up than
anyone else and after a few casts hooked the only fish I saw caught
during our stay.

Admittedly it's impossible to isolate the effect of the change
of fly since I flawed the experiment by also altering the presentation. Nonetheless it illustrates how a drastic shift in approach may
move a bead on the abacus.

The tradition supporting the edifice of the "classic" salmon
fly is so varied and fascinating that many books in different periods
have traced its development. Several of these works are listed in
the bibliography and I have no intention of treading on such well-
seeded pastures. But I included Figure 16 to illustrate the various
components of a classic fly so you'll be thinking only of fishing
when the talk turns to shoulders and butts. One confusing usage
involving hair-wing flies has a tag occasionally referred to as a butt.
In any event, you will rarely see anyone using a fully dressed classic
featherwing pattern in the streams of North America, although
"reduced versions" of these colorful flies are still found in many
an angler's box. "Reduced version" means that some of the components are dropped and the exotic feathers, like Indian crow,
toucan, bustard, and blue chatterer, are replaced by readily available
materials.

Many early North American salmon anglers came from Britain
and were partial to the patterns used at home. Despite that, flies
were developed locally and others accompanied travelers from the
U.S. Unfortunately, writers of the period were brief in their descriptions and seldom left drawings of flies they used. However, we
can infer from writers like Lanman (1856), Dashwood (1871), and
Hallock (1890) that simple hackle patterns or those with only a wool
body and plain feather wing were effective. Dashwood gives one
dressing from a fly tier in Saint John, New Brunswick, named after

TABLE 2. PARTRIDGE SALMON HOOKS

M — Single Salmon Hooks
The traditional salmon iron.

CS10 — Bartleet Salmon Fly Hooks
Excellent hooking features for all types
of salmon & steelhead flies.

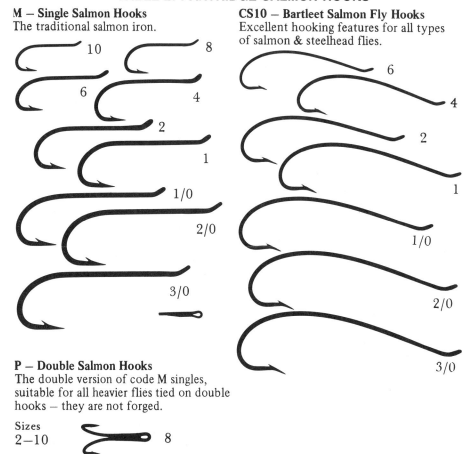

P — Double Salmon Hooks
The double version of code M singles,
suitable for all heavier flies tied on double
hooks — they are not forged.

Sizes
2–10   8

its creator, the Nicholson. It had brown mallard wings with a few
strands of golden pheasant neck feathers underneath and a fiery
brown body wound with blue and claret hackle.

What flies should you have to start? It's fair to say there are
a half-dozen patterns in such wide use that I recommend them for
any excursion. While this isn't a fly-tying text, it's reasonable to
provide recipes and tying instructions for this basic selection. I have
also included a few recipes for flies that have some historical
significance. The other side of your box should represent the recommendations of the lodge or a fly-fishing shop near your destination. While it's difficult to be tying flies at the last minute, you

TABLE 2. (Continued)

N – Single Low Water Hooks
For traditional low water salmon and steelhead flies.

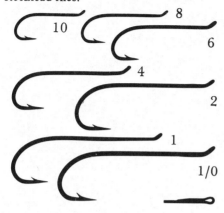

O1 – Single Wilson Hooks
A beautiful traditional hook for salmon and steelhead dry flies.

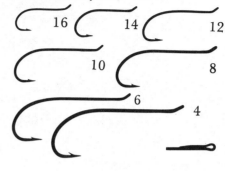

Q – Double Low Water Hooks
These are the double version of code N low water hooks.

Sizes
2–10

8

O2 – Double Wilson Hooks
Identical to O1 but in double form. A very strong but light weight double with excellent hooking qualities.

Sizes
4–14

8

should still try to get the most recent information, making the call no more than a week before your arrival.

Before discussing the individual patterns, a few notes on the general proportions of normal hair wings which are usually adhered to by most tiers. Referring to Figure 17, they are as follows:

Tag: Three turns beginning directly above the barb.
Tip: Between end of the tag and a line drawn vertically from the point of the hook.
Tail: Extends to end of the hook bend.
Butt: Over hook point.
Body: From butt to beginning of looped eye.
Wing: Even with tip of the tail.
Throat Hackle: Three-quarters to point of hook.
Palmer Rib: Width of hook gape.
Tinsel Rib: Five turns.
Shoulder: One-third length of wing.
Head: Small, neat, and lacquered.

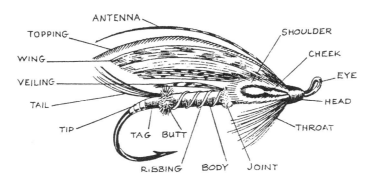

FIGURE 16. Parts of A Classic Salmon Fly

THE PATTERNS

The Bomber

The small group of travelers clustered together as if community offered some protection from the peering eyes of the curious and the predators. Twenty feet upstream of the bridge across the North Branch of the Renous River, in three feet of water, they chose to wait out the day exposed.

They were waiting when our 4x4 pulled off the road onto some flat ground dotted by tough scrubby bushes. Less sturdy vegetation had succumbed to the tires of the hundreds of cars, campers, and trailers that had stopped there over the years. The three of us got out to take a look. It was late morning and the resident crowd had put the contents of several fly boxes over the reluctant salmon. No one had had any success. As I watched the salmon sway side to side in the current, I wondered why they hadn't chosen to hold in the deeper pool just thirty feet closer to the ocean.

One by one our trio of anglers moved through the run to the rhythms of the cast and the advice of the assembled onlookers on the bridge. After several passes both groups gave up. Time for a noontime snack and siesta. Intrigued as always by unmovable fish, I dug out a trout rod and returned to float a number 16 Haystack over their heads. No interest. Just for fun I knotted on a number 4 Bomber. Some fun! The 4X tippet rebelled vigorously but I wasn't in the mood to cut back a good trout leader for such silliness.

Oh oh! A grilse just followed that monstrosity for ten feet until it started to drag. Reflexively I dumped another cast upstream and he rose swiftly to the fly as it passed over his head. Sadly, the knot was weak, resulting in another long release. For the next half-hour the grilse did a fair imitation of Katerina Witt in an attempt to shake loose the hunk of white deerhair stuck in its jaw.

Something special about this ineptness, you ask? Salmon are known to find Bombers quite attractive. Well, I checked later and learned that a number of folks had presented a variety of similar flies to those fish earlier in the morning. Was it the simply the old story of the two hundred and first cast? Or was it because, probably for the first time that day, the bridge and banks were virtually unoccupied? Human forms, save for mine, were absent from the salmon's view. But let's not forget the fly.

It's no exaggeration to say that this iconoclastic floater has a worldwide reputation. Bombers are offered to large brown trout in Finland and New Zealand, steelhead in North America, Atlantic salmon in Canada and Britain, and who know what and where else outside my ken.

Unlike with many, the history of this fly wasn't lost in the mists of an early morning on a salmon river. The creator of the Bomber died only recently in Prince William, New Brunswick. The Reverend Elmer J. Smith moved to the Miramichi area from Maine in the late 1960's, having already fished its rivers for many years. Contrary to expectations, his innovation was not developed as a salmon fly.

Reverend Smith explained to me a few years ago: ''I was living in Portland, Maine, in the late fifties. During a visit to my close friend Herb Johnson — who created the Herb Johnson Special — we decided to fish the Royal River in Yarmouth for large sea-run browns one evening. Along came a young kid with some rudimentary fly tackle. He threw out a big hair mouse and hooked a brown trout that went around 8 or 9 pounds. I decided to try and develop a fly with similar characteristics that was easier to tie and cast.

''The original fly isn't cigar-shaped. It has a slight taper toward the eye but is more or less cylindrical. I use two high-quality Metz hackles tied in by the butts. In the beginning the fly had calftail at the front as well as the back but I've recently dropped the forward clump as unnecessary.''

(A to D) Bomber

Of course no really good fly could be tied with ordinary materials. Reverend Smith used Herter Gaelic Supreme hooks, and the hackles were forty-five years old when I spoke to him. They were six to eight inches long with very little change in width; he dyed them himself. In his words, ''the fly was intended to be fished downstream with drag. I wanted a new style of fly, a commotion fly. I believe that the stiffness of the hackle is important. It's the penetration of the surface that makes it attractive. Remember, it floats on the deerhair body, not the hackle.'' The slight taper toward the eye was designed to make the pick-up easier.

Often there is an interesting story behind a fly's name. Not so with the Bomber. It wasn't any more complicated than the chance remark of a friend to Rev. Smith: ''That's a real bomb, isn't it?'' Come to think of it, the shape of the deerhair body is reminiscent of the payloads of World War II Flying Forts. Such a simple but graphic name was unlikely to be original. Joe Bates's book, *Atlantic Salmon Flies and Fishing* (1970), gives a wet-fly pattern of the same name created by Joe Aucoin of Nova Scotia in the 1920's. There are also several trout flies with an identical moniker.

The Bomber in its largest incarnations is as well known for the fish it hasn't hooked as for those it has. A well-earned reputation for inciting piscine aggravation makes it a good choice for a searching pattern. A fish that reacts to a large Bomber may well be taken on a smaller fly.

No Atlantic salmon fisher of my acquaintance would come to the river without a supply of Bombers. The fly is even beginning to show its mettle during the early spring season on the Miramichi. Fished dead-drift, or riffling across downstream, the Bomber's effectiveness will continue to produce outstanding memories for its disciples.

Bomber

Hook: Mustad 9671 or 9672, sizes 2 to 8. Partridge has recently introduced a new Bomber Hook (CS42) which is virtually identical to the Wilson Dry Fly except for a turned-down looped eye. My first impression, however, is that the curved rear portion of the shank would make it a better Buck Bug hook, although another interpretation would suggest using it to produce a low-water version of the Bomber.

Thread: Black or white Kevlar.

Tying Instructions:

1. Attach the thread over the point of the hook. Put a drop of cement on the thread to keep it from slipping. Tie in a bunch of calftail to extend beyond the bend the length of the hook gape. Cement the winding.
2. Clip the calftail close to the thread. Begin spinning clumps of deerhair on the bare hook.
3. Spin deerhair clumps to within 1/8 inch of the eye. Half-hitch the thread four or five times and cut. Remove the fly from the vise and clip to shape.
4. Put the fly back in the vise and reattach the thread at the rear over the tail winds. Tie in the hackle(s) by the *stem* and wind the thread through the body to the front. Select a slightly smaller clump of calftail than that used for the tail and tie it in lying forward over the eye. A few winds in front of the wing will help lift it away from the eye. Put a drop of cement on the winds, clip the excess calftail, and then palmer the hackle(s) forward. Tie off behind the wing, whip finish, and cement the windings.

Notes:

1. Breaking the thread when spinning deerhair is very aggravating. I use Kevlar which never breaks. Some people report that it can cut the hair, but when using coarse deerhair I rarely have any trouble.
2. Start with a clump of deerhair about half the size of a pencil and push it very gently up against the tail windings. Even using cement, those windings are a little fragile. Spin the largest manageable clumps until almost reaching the front and then switch back to smaller ones to ensure there is enough space left for the wing.
3. Start clipping the body from the front. I use regular and then curved serrated scissors. When approaching the tail get your fingers under the flared hair at the back to grip the tie-in point. Clip carefully around this point. Leaving some short deerhair stubs at the tail will cover the windings.
4. With most available saddle hackle you will be hard-pressed on larger flies to get constant width winds from the tail to the head. While you could tie off one hackle and start another in the middle of the body, this isn't fully satisfactory.
5. As best I can determine, a number 2 Herter Gaelic Supreme is the same as a Mustad 9672 and similar hooks by other manufacturers.

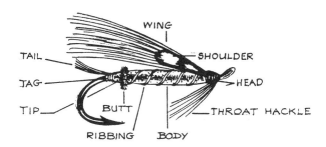

FIGURE 17. Proportions of a hairwing Atlantic salmon fly

The Buck Bug

Unquestionably the most popular fly on the salmon rivers of eastern Canada is the Buck Bug (often called simply Bug) and its many variations, in particular the Green Machine and most recently the Glitter Bug. There is even a blue version, originated by the crowd at Quarryville (a popular junction pool of the main Miramichi and Renous rivers) which has been dubbed, not surprisingly, the Smurf.

There seems to be confusion over who originated the Buck Bug, but I believe it was Joe Carter of Moncton, New Brunswick. I think a fly should be named after its creator, but unfortunately the name Buck Bug is so firmly entrenched that a change is impossible. Because the fly is so close in design to its natural parent, the Bomber, it might not deserve a separate name were it not for the important difference in the way it is presently fished. The first Buck Bugs I tossed were intended to be used dry or wet, but over the years the body has been slimmed down and it is primarily fished downstream as a wet fly today.

Buck Bug

Hook: Mustad 3908, sizes 4 to 8.
Tip or Butt: fluorescent wool, color to suit your taste but red and green are the most popular.
Body: spun deerhair.
Hackle: cock's hackle, usually brown or orange.
Note: I used to tie this fly with a natural deerhair tail and no tip, but this has gone out of fashion.

Tying Instructions: Tied like the Bomber with the obvious adjustments. As the photo shows, the deerhair body is trimmed closer to the hook.

To tie the Green Machine simply use deer hair of a color described by Jerry Doak as a "blend of both Green Highlander and Insect Green dyes." The best source of the material is Jerry's shop (address at the end of the chapter). The hackle is orange. For the Glitterbug, add a tail of four strands of Krystal Flash just forward of the tip (or drop the tip). Keep the tail short; it should not extend beyond the bend of the hook. You can pick the color of Krystal Flash to suit your personality, although Pearlescent is a favorite. Any version of the Buck Bug may be jazzed up in this fashion.

The Cosseboom

I don't know if every salmon angler thinks as I do, but I have a favorite fly, one that seems to come through for me when the chips are down. It's the Cosseboom. There is really no rhyme or reason for the choice — it isn't that different from many other flies — but I bend it on with unreasoned confidence. I even carry one around in my wallet so that regardless of the situation, I will have one close at hand. According to Joe Bates, one of the great students and raconteurs of North American Atlantic salmon fishing history, the Cosseboom Special, now called simply Cosseboom, was originally tied by John Cosseboom and used on Nova Scotia's Margaree River in 1923. There are a number of other flies in the Cosseboom series but to my knowledge only the original, as tied below, remains popular.

Just before this chapter was written, on a trip to the Dungarvon River in New Brunswick, I was gratified to watch a friend catch and release his first salmon on a Cosseboom. That he had it in his box, or tied it on, was no accident considering the build-up I had given the fly.

The dressing, after Bates, is as follows:

Cosseboom

Hook: Partridge or Mustad Salmon, single or double, sizes 4/0 to 10.

Tag: Embossed silver tinsel in a suitable width for the size of the hook.

Tail: Green floss (see color plate) or if you have access to Pearsall's floss it's shade #82.

Body: Floss, as for the tail.

Ribbing: Embossed silver tinsel.

Wing: Small bunch of grey squirrel-tail hair extending no farther than the end of the tail.

Hackle: Lemon-yellow tied on as a collar after the wing is applied and slanted rearward to merge with the top of the wing.

Head: Red.

The original pattern gives Jungle Cock cheeks as optional but they are rarely seen today.

The Oriole

Perhaps this fly doesn't deserve to be included in a box purporting to contain today's most popular flies, but only a soulless angler could exclude the pattern that killed his first large salmon. Occasionally it still takes a fish or two but I can't claim it's a consistent producer. On the other hand, I was heartened to hear during a recent visit to Doak's, arguably the best and best-known salmon-fishing tackle shop in Canada, that an angler had released an exceptional salmon which came to an Oriole tied many years ago by the shop's founder, Wally Doak.

The Oriole is one of the many patterns developed by Ira Gruber, who, in the late 1930's, created a number of effective salmon flies and is sometimes credited with originating the distinctive Miramichi style of tying. This style calls for a slim, cigar-shaped body, fine tinsel ribbing, low-set wing, and sparse throat hackle.

Oriole

What follows is the original dressing of this pattern as described by Bates.

Hook: Partridge or Mustad Salmon, sizes 4 to 10, may also be tied low-water.

Tail: A few fibers from the red body feather of a golden pheasant.

Body: Black floss or wool, cigar-shaped.

Ribbing: Fine oval silver tinsel, with two turns taken under the
tail, as a tag.
Hackle: Brown, two or three turns of which are wound on as a
collar and pulled down before the wing is applied. The fibers
extend two-thirds of the way to the point of the hook.
Wing: Underwing — several fibers of the brown-red body feather
of a golden pheasant. Overwing — in four sections, two on
each side, of grey mallard dyed green drake color, tied low
to hug the body.
Head: Black.

The Butterfly

The St. Mary's River is considered an early river, fishing well
in June and early July. Like many Nova Scotia rivers it suffers badly
from drought conditions brought on, I believe, by obscene clear-
cut logging practices. Recently it seems that early closure happens
more and more often.

Some years ago I took a novice to the river to introduce him
to the sport. The weather was beautiful and we drove well up the
river to enjoy the countryside. Arriving at the chosen pool, we
found three anglers already moving down through the riffle so we
walked to the top and took our places in the rotation. After ten
minutes or so, a large red-haired gentleman at the front of the queue
hooked a grilse. The salmon played well, jumping three or four
times, but got off after about five minutes. At this point the air colored and the guy threw his rod into the water and then kicked it
up onto the shingle, breaking it in the process. His companions,
who had, in the accepted fashion, reeled up their lines to avoid
fouling, appeared so chagrined at the behavior of their friend that
they took him away.

After several minutes of shock at what we had just witnessed,
I resumed casting and shortly killed a grilse on a Butterfly. I can
honestly say, however, that the experience was marred by the recent outrage and we soon left.

The Butterfly has always been a favorite of mine. Along the
Miramichi system during the late sixties and early seventies, it was
as fashionable as mini-skirts. The fly didn't travel all that well and
today has dropped into fifth or sixth place in the popularity polls

on its home waters. My experiences with the Butterfly suggest that it works best in fast, riffly sections which gives the wings plenty of action. This type of water is primarily inhabited by grilse.

The reason I'm still so keen on the Butterfly is that it presents a substantially different profile to the salmon from the standard hair-wing style. The twin white wings, tied in a rakish angle somewhat like a downwing caddis imitation, create activity in the water. The Butterfly was originated circa 1956 by Maurice Ingalls, a Floridian fishing in the Blackville, New Brunswick, area. The genesis of the design is clearly a white-winged coachman which incorporates what I consider to be the most effective fly-tying material of all time, peacock herl.

Butterfly

Hook: Partridge or Mustad Salmon, sizes 4 to 10, single or double, sometimes tied low-water.

Tail: A dozen or so fibers of a bright red hackle, fairly long.

Body: Wound with rusty peacock herl.

Wing: A divided wing of white goat hair, slightly longer than the body and set a bit above the body, slanted backward at an angle of about 45 degrees. The wings are very sparse and the hair should be from a small goat, as the hair from large goats is too brittle and too stiff.

Hackle: Two turns of a brown hackle wound on as a collar, one turn behind the wings and one in front. The hackle is about half as long as the wing hair, is applied dry-fly style, and should be very sparse.

Notes:

Rusty-colored peacock herl is not easily found and most Butterflys are tied with the more available bronze color. Some tiers also substitute calftail, or calf bodyhair for the goat.

Green Butt (Black Bear)

Possibly the fly with the most sustained popularity on many of eastern Canada's salmon rivers is this simple pattern tied in a number of variations. Some of the variants have names (e.g., Con-

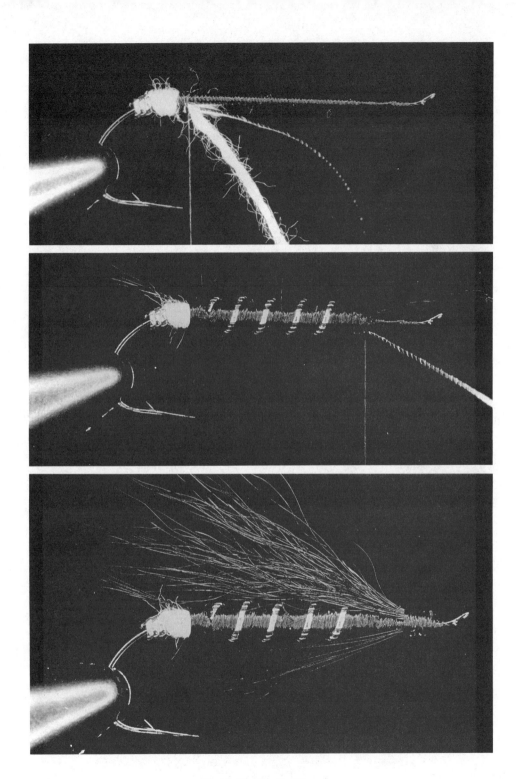

(A to C) Black Bear

rad and Undertaker) but in reality they are all cast from the same mold. The distinguishing features of the breed are a prominent colored butt (as mentioned earlier, an unfortunate departure from standard nomenclature — I would call this a tip), a slim dark body, and a dark, low-set, hair wing.

Perhaps because of its simplicity or widespread popularity, trying to pin down a patent pattern is a nightmare. Bates, whom I usually consider to be authoritative, gives a pattern called the Black Bear in *Atlantic Salmon Flies and Fishing* (1970) that he says was originally dressed by Harry Smith of Maine in the 1920's. With its tail of quill, no butt, no ribbing, and a throat of bear hair instead of hackle, it is a far cry from the modern version. However, he does say that the "butt" series may also have come from an Ira Gruber dressing called the Black Spider originating around 1935. I would agree, as the pattern is very close to what is tied today. Unfortunately, in his later tour de force, *The Art of the Atlantic Salmon Fly* (1987), Bates ignores the Gruber connection and adds some strange stuff to the Smith pattern (like a floss tail). The result bears no resemblance to what you would find on the Miramichi.

Just to touch on the additional confusion, here is what others say about this fly, Dick Stewart and Farrow Allen in *Flies for Atlantic Salmon* (1991) gave it a silver rib and golden pheasant topping tail. Poul Jorgensen's *Salmon Flies* (1978) follows Bates for the Black Bear but gives a separate pattern for the Green Butt including a white silk base for the green floss butt, a golden pheasant tail and silver rib. Fulsher and Krom, in *Hair-Wing Atlantic Salmon Flies* (1981), call for gold tinsel and a tail of black hackle fibers. They consider the silver tinsel version to be the Conrad. Finally, in *The Atlantic Salmon Fly, The Tyers and Their Art* (1991) by Judith Dunham, a well-known New Brunswick tier introduced a hackle color, black grizzly, that I've never seen called up on any fly, let alone a salmon fly.

As a morose aside, I note that while Green Butts have accounted for many of the grilse I've killed over the years, no large salmon has ever succumbed to its charms. In any event, here is the dressing I learned and fish with. It's the same as that of Fulsher and Krom, supported by Eric Leiser in *The Book of Fly Patterns* (1987).

Green Butt (Black Bear)

Hook: Partridge or Mustad Salmon, single or double, sizes 2
   to 10 (tied low-water as well).
Tag: Oval gold tinsel.
Tip (Butt): Fluorescent green wool or floss (see plate for color).
Tail: Black hackle fibers.
Body: Black floss/wool, or peacock herl (modern).
Rib: Oval gold tinsel.
Hackle: Black, tied in as a throat.
Wing: Black bear hair, tied sparse.
Head: Black.

The Rusty Rat

I'd like to recount some personal successes with this pattern
but the truth is it's included because it's a favorite on Quebec rivers
and the Restigouche, places I rarely (or in the case of the latter,
never) fish. Jean-Paul Dube suggests the Rusty Rat gained many
adherents after it captivated a forty-six pound salmon in the
Matapedia. I've carried a few in my box for many years because
you never know where you'll be next week but I recall only a couple of grilse that it's killed. Can't blame the pattern though; it's
hard to shine when you rarely see the sun.

There is an interesting scandal brewing over the originator of
the Rusty Rat. Bates attributes the pattern to a Dr. Orrin Summers
of New Jersey — a neighbor of Herbert Howard who tied the first
Rat (the Grey Rat) and named it for Roy Angus Thompson, who
suggested the wing material. There is another claim on behalf of
the curmudgeonly J.C. (Clovie) Arsenault of Atholville, a famous
tier of the Restigouche area. Folklore has it that Bates held a grudge
against Arsenault because the latter refused to donate flies for the
former's book, and it's true that Arsenault's name does not appear in Bate's book, a pointed omission.

Rusty Rat
(pattern after Bates)

Hook: Partridge or Mustad Salmon, single or double, sizes 6/0
   to 10.
Tag: Oval gold tinsel.

Tail: Three or four peacock sword feathers, tied in rather short.
Body: Rear half, bright yellow floss; forward half, peacock herl.
  A length of the yellow floss extends as a veiling from the
  middle of the body nearly to the end of the body on top of
  the fly.
Ribbing: Oval gold tinsel.
Wing: A small bunch of the guard hairs of a gray fox.
Hackle: A grizzly hackle tied on as a collar and slanted
  rearward.
Head: Red.

The Blue Charm

The Blue Charm is the only classic pattern, albeit in a hairwing version, that I carry. Blue has been established as the color that retains its visibility the longest as the water gets deeper and the Blue Charm is popular throughout eastern Canada as well as on the salmon rivers of Britain and Iceland.

It's a strange coincidence that this fly, which is one of the few to survive a century (at least in North America), is also one about which little is known of its origin. Searching through numerous references revealed only that it probably was first dressed by an unknown tier in the last few decades of the nineteenth century who lived around the Dee River of Scotland. It gained considerable prominence from being a favorite fly of A.H.E. Wood for his greased line system. The pattern given below is the hairwing version popular in North America.

Blue Charm

Hook: Partridge or Mustad Salmon, often in low water form,
  sizes 4 to 10.
Tag: Fine oval silver tinsel.
Tip: Yellow floss.
Tail: Golden pheasant crest.
Body: Black floss.
Rib: Oval silver tinsel.
Throat: Deep blue hackle.
Wing: Gray squirrel tail.

Now for something a bit surprising. If you glance back over the patterns I've recommended you'll see that they are all essentially drab. Not a tinsel-bodied fly among them. The reason is that I succeed or fail in dirty water, or whenever a flashy body seems appropriate, on the back of a Marabou Muddler. My largest salmon and several runners-up (all unweighed because they were taken in catch and release waters) have come to this killer in chartreuse, black, and red. In colored water I bend on a chartreuse first, followed by a black if that fails. Even though the recipe is found in almost every fly tying book published, I'll risk accusations of padding for the sake of completeness.

The Marabou Muddler

Hook: Mustad 79850, sizes 2 to 10.
Tail: Small clump of red hackle with a bunch of marabou over.
Body: Mylar tinsel; or tinsel chenille; or mylar tubing, in both gold and silver.
Wing: Marabou.
Collar: Spun deerbody hair; try not to use hair that is too soft because in my view it is essential that the collar flare out from the body.
Head: Spun deerbody hair clipped into a bullet shape but flat on the bottom.

Having floated a boxful of dry flies over various salmon during the years, I've convinced myself, perhaps because of a slothful nature, that if a salmon won't rise to some size or color of Bomber, Buck Bug, or Wulff, then it's too sulky for me. Although, as noted above, Lee Wulff did some grandstanding with #24 hooks, I don't fish anything smaller than #12. When angling on public water, once you get down to those light-wire trout hooks you're likely to start pricking more salmon than is acceptable. Again for the sake of completeness, here's the recipe for the White Wulff (other colors are simple variations).

The White Wulff

Hook: Mustad 90240 or Wilson Dry Fly.
Tail: Bunch of white calftail.

Body: White or cream wool.
Wings: White calftail, tied upright and divided.
Hackle: Badger.

ON CHOOSING A FLY

Much has been made, and much more will be, about how to
choose the fly. In Britain they start with size and have published
charts which give the ''correct'' size based on the temperature of
the water. The warmer the water the smaller the fly. Most salmon
fishers would agree that this is generally correct, although there
is plenty of contrary experience. Some expert anglers suggest changing sizes with water speed. For example, suppose you believe that
a size 6 is appropriate for the temperature. They would recommend
beginning with a size 4 in the fast water at the head of the pool,
changing to a 6 as the current slowed in the middle, and then bend-
ing on a 4 again if the water picked up speed in the tail. As is the
case with most things about fishing, this advice is hardly new. Sir
Humphrey Davy in *Salmonia* (1828) suggested the same approach.

Because we rarely start fishing in North America until the water
has warmed considerably, large flies (below size 2) are today reserved for high, cold water in the fall. The most common size
throughout the season is a number 6. Move down to 8's and 10's
if the water is low and warm, or experiment with low-water ties.

Pattern selection is another story. Some anglers have experimented with using a single pattern for a whole season, notably
A.H.E. Wood (March Brown) and Frank Griswold (Griswold Gray),
and claim to have maintained their usual average. Most of us aren't
prepared to go that far and besides it would be boring. Conversely,
toting twenty boxes filled with hundreds of patterns is ludicrous.
A half dozen wet fly dressings in various sizes is plenty. However,
I wouldn't be without a supply of whatever is recommended by
a lodge or tackle shop in the area I'm visiting. So even if you start
with a ''standard'' selection, you will build up a collection after
a few trips to different rivers.

There are some old saws such as ''bright day, bright fly — dark
day, dark fly.'' This may well be a good guide but my experience

suggests that dark wet flies are most successful in the rivers I fish (although how to class something like a Butterfly with its white wing is a problem). As previously mentioned, I switch to Marabou Muddlers when fishing deep or in colored water. The situation is best summed up by Eric Travener in *Fly Tying for Salmon* (1947): "But the last thing I should expect to find in any solution is completeness and simplicity, or that one explanation will cover all the difficulties with which, to our endless delight, the whole problem bristles."

Bill Ensor tells a great story about an experienced angler who liked to carry dozens of patterns stuck to the outside of his hat. One day after a long walk to a pool he met a young fellow coming up the path carrying his daily limit of two grilse. To no one's surprise, after the usual pleasantries, the critical question was posed: "What did you get them on?" The successful angler stared at the festooned fedora for a few moments and replied, "You've got one."

I tie most of my salmon flies, but what I buy I get from W.W. Doak. Obviously there are other quality suppliers but I can recommend Jerry Doak's operation without reservation: W.W. Doak, P.O. Box 95, Doaktown, N.B., Canada E0C 1G0.

Releasing a salmon on the St. John River, N.B.

Fish from the tail — MSW Miramichi River

Working down the Run — angler on left may be too deep

Salmon hooked downstream of brook — Cains River, N.B.

Grilse from tail of a small pool — Dungarvon River

A good-sized cotton mesh net

Into the turn

A drove of salmon (Jack Swedberg photo)

Keeping a grilse out of the bushes — NW Miramichi River
(Jim Marriner Photo)

Sylvia Bashline playing salmon on Dungarvon River (Bill Ensor photo)

Follow that fish — MSW Miramichi River

Netting by yourself (Jack Swedberg photo)

Swimming for dry land — Margaree River

Orderly Rotation — Margaree River

Stewiacke River, N.S.

CHAPTER 9

HOOKING, PLAYING, AND LANDING

For many years I rarely lost a salmon. Sure I had my share of plucks and pulls, but once on the hook, they came ashore. Then, as if I had unknowingly irritated a vengeful spirit, luck turned on me like a rabid dog. Knots came undone, flies pulled out, salmon wrapped themselves up in the leader like sharks, and leaders wound around snags. Thankfully, before I quit in frustration, things got back to normal. Apparently you can do everything right and still come up short, but here are a few tips to improve the odds.

HOOKING

Possibly the second most perplexing of all subjects in salmon fishing (after the choice of fly), hooking technique has generated considerable debate during the almost one hundred years that floating lines have been used. It's never been a matter of contention when using deeply sunk lines and 4/0 flies because by the time you feel anything the salmon is probably on (or off). You need only strike hard to sink that big iron deeper into its jaw. But once the action moved close to the surface the situation changed. Quick strikes usually meant lost fish, so anglers ran the gamut from giving a yard of more of slack line to continuing to cross their eyes. What follows is a summary of what has already been said in the chapters on techniques.

> **Rule 1:** If the fly is fishing downstream with little or no slack and a salmon takes, do nothing; the salmon will hook itself. More fish are lost by beginners because they strike when seeing a rise than for any other reason. At the end of the first run either carry on or strike. Some strike, on the theory that if the salmon is lightly hooked they prefer to lose it early on. I, on the other hand, am an optimist, and hope that I can land a delicately attached fish.

The only exception to Rule 1 is when the fly is at the dangle, immediately below you. This is the hardest position in which to hook any fish and what you do probably won't matter much. The only time I can remember a salmon following my fly right to shore was many years ago at Wasson's Bar. I hooked up but I have no idea what I did. An appealing theory is to drop the rod quickly if you feel a tug or see a swirl. This puts a little slack in the line so that the fish can turn. Then strike and hope.

Rule 2: If there is slack line on the water up or across stream, strike. Ah, but when? is the question. The answer depends on how much slack is hanging about. With sixty feet of squiggles, leading to an upstream dry fly, get on it immediately. In close, hold off until you see the salmon disappear. When fishing a slack-line sunk fly (like the Patent or upstream nymph) do it with gusto.

FIGHTING

Techniques for handling large fish are well known. Never give a sucker (or a salmon) an even break. Here's how:

1. If the banks are clear, get to shore as quickly as possible. Play the salmon off the reel and keep the pressure on at all times — babying a salmon is unsportsmanlike. Do not let the rod point at the fish and *keep your hands away from the reel handle when the fish is running.* The instant the salmon stops running, regain line by "pumping." Put the butt of the rod against your belly and reel in while pivoting the rod toward the fish. Then clamp the reel and pull the rod back to its original position. Be prepared to release the reel should the fish decide to run again.

2. Try and stay even with or below the fish. If it's running downstream, so are you, taking up slack as you go. Most of the time if the salmon is hooked in a riffle or run and decides to go, it heads downstream for the first bit of quiet water. Usually, but certainly not always, it won't go over the thin water at the end of the tail and you will get to slug it out in the pool. Don't follow

(A to C) Tailing a salmon sequence (Jack Swedberg photos)

the lead of certain nineteenth-century anglers who, according to Charles Lanman, jumped into swift, rocky rivers to get around obstacles on the bank and then swam to shore! Should you be unable to follow a salmon downstream, try the tactic mentioned in Chapter 6 — release line from the reel so that the line will bag below the fish. This may induce the salmon to run back upstream. Another tactic for moving a salmon upstream to escape trouble is "the walk." With as straight a line as possible, clamp the reel and walk steadily upstream. In many cases the fish will follow obediently.

3. Don't attempt to lift the fish out of the water! Rather, apply side strain whenever you can while keeping the line out of the water. Besides tiring the salmon more quickly, it reduces its tendency to jump. (Note: This does not conflict with the advice to keep the rod tip up, which is really meant to prevent anglers from pointing the rod at the fish.) When there is a lot of line out, it is best to keep as much of it above the surface as possible — preventing the line from being "drowned," which can put considerable pressure on the leader and fly. This requires keeping the rod tip high. Be ready to wind up whenever the fish yields to the pressure. Good luck if it streaks toward you at full speed!

4. Bowing to the fish, or dropping the rod when it jumps, is a waste of time if there is lots of line on the water but it probably won't hurt. If a salmon jumps in close and all the line is in the air, you could be in trouble if you don't give it some slack.

5. A tired salmon in close should make you as nervous as a first kiss. If you can get the fish near enough to land without bringing any knots past the tip guide, do so. If not, reel up. I watched an angler on the St. John River almost kill a salmon because he was afraid to reel up, a gruesome performance. Should the salmon take off when the knot is past the tip guide, drop the rod tip; the knot will usually clear. This has always worked for me.

6. What to do with a sulking salmon? If side strain won't budge it, try hitting the butt of the rod with a rock, giving the fish some slack, throwing a rock or two into the pool — *only if you are alone!* — or, as a last resort, going downstream and hand-lining. If it's

a really big salmon and you are in private water or alone, I might be tempted (this has never happened to me) to reduce the strain to a minimum and wait it out.

LANDING

There are three ways to land a salmon: hand-tailing, netting, or beaching. A fourth way, with a tailer, has fallen into disfavor even though you might see one from time to time on the river.

Hand-Tailing

The area just ahead of a salmon's tail is known as the wrist. A grilse's wrist is less developed and harder to grab than a large salmon's, but it's still possible. Once the salmon is tired, re-enter the water if you have been fighting it from shore. Hold the rod above the grip (don't trap the line) to shorten the distance and push it behind you. Reach down slowly and grip the wrist firmly — a wool or cotton glove is a welcome aid. This seems to freeze most fish although there will be exceptions. Now slip your other hand under the salmon's belly and lift gently until reaching the surface if a picture is the object, but don't lift the fish completely out of the water. Then grip and twist the fly for an easy release. It's best to do this in a couple feet of water because salmon get very skittish when brought into the shallows.

Netting

Netting is the best way to safely land a salmon when fishing with a companion — and the easiest too, if done properly. The netter is responsible for only one thing — lifting the net when the fish is over the top. The angler is responsible for everything else. The net should be big and made with cotton mesh so as not to damage the fish. Place a few stones in the bottom to keep the mesh from billowing up. Then the netter stays absolutely still, preferably downstream of the fish and in about three feet of water. Hold the net about a foot below the surface with the front of the rim angled downward. The angler brings the salmon over the top of the net and the netter lifts. No jabbing, stabbing, or other foolishness. I don't recommend single-handed netting although it's certainly possible. A large enough net is awkward to carry and difficult to manage alone, although many British anglers seem to cope — and with long two-handed rods to boot.

Beaching

I've beached many salmon and never lost one. To do it properly the area must have a gradual slope of gravel, grass, or small stones, and have enough room for you to back up. Once the fish is tired and you can start to lead it to shore, bring the line in until there is fifteen feet outside the tip. Now, holding the rod horizontal and pointing downstream, without reeling, back steadily up the beach. The salmon will almost always follow obediently. Once the salmon's belly touches the gravel move more quickly and keep it coming at least ten feet inland.

If you have very little room behind you, or if the beach is rugged, then you have problems. Turning sideways and moving the rod inland may work but it's touch and go. Better to wade out and try to tail the fish.

Killing

Traditionally, you didn't catch a salmon, you killed it. Today, with catch-and-release a major factor in our salmon fishing, the phrase is a bit unfortunate. However, if you intend to keep a salmon, then kill it quickly. A wooden priest is a good tool but in a pinch a rock will do. All that's required is a sharp blow on the top of the head.

To keep a salmon fresh, do not gut it immediately. Build a small rock pool (cradle) at the shoreline so that the fish is kept underwater. Then when you are ready to return to camp, clean the fish and keep it cool. Most anglers scale salmon during cleaning.

Two anglers sharing a short stretch of holding water on the LaHave River, N.S.

Bill Ensor about to release a fine Upsalquitch River salmon (Doug Haney photo)

CHAPTER 10

ETHICS AND ETIQUETTE

Today, only our native peoples should be found fishing a salmon river primarily for food (and only for their own consumption). For the rest of us it's a sport. Yes, there are regulations designed to conserve the species, but there are only ethics to conserve the sport. While thinking that the old days were somehow better is usually dismissed as nostalgia, there seems to be considerable truth in the feeling where salmon rivers are concerned. The rampant and politically encouraged greed of the 1980's has found its way to our rivers.

I recently learned of an incident on one of the few unlimited public-access waters in Quebec. It was invaded by a group of ignorant jerks who decided to control the pool by arriving before dawn and taking up stands. They wouldn't move and apparently felt, like a gang, that their numbers would intimidate other anglers into leaving them to their games. It took a call to the local group that controls the river to get them to move on.

You will encounter two vastly different situations on a salmon pool depending on where you fish. In order to comfortably accommodate the often large number of anglers that congregate at popular public pools, a code of behavior is necessary. Even if you cast over a private pool, there are courtesies that must be observed. I'll begin by describing the not insubstantial code concerning rotation.

ROTATION

Rotating a pool is the system used to give everyone an equal chance to fish. Here are the salient points:

1. Each angler takes a turn moving through the pool. The first angler to arrive has the right to move through the pool first. *Never go in front of another angler.*

As they say in legalese, notwithstanding the generality of the foregoing, there are two exceptions to Rule 1. If the preceding angler continues fishing well past where the others are leaving the pool, you can retire at that point and expect to take over his place which he forfeited by going too far downstream. This of course applies to you as well. Note that even if you want to fish the far end of pool, for example with a dry fly, you should still start at the top of the rotation. Yes, you will encounter even experienced hands that bend this rule, but you shouldn't.

The second situation is one that I encountered on the Margaree River several years ago. It was on a long pool that I found myself sharing with two first-time anglers. They had already started by the time I got there and were about halfway down the pool. I started at the head of the run but soon discovered they had feet of concrete, and before long I was right behind them. After a few minutes of no movement, I reeled in and explained rotation to them. I also explained that by not moving they were missing opportunities and that ten or fifteen casts in the same spot was inefficient. They were polite and started to move but after a few casts they became riveted again. This time I had to tell them that I was going to move in front of them and so went 50 yards downstream. During the next hour I hooked two large salmon, while they continued to cast from the same spot. Even so, I still felt badly about moving in front; years of conditioning are difficult to overcome, I guess.

2. Step into the pool in turn. If you want to begin with short casts to cover the close-in water, move in a little sooner, but on no account let your fly drift in front of the preceding angler. Another way to cut down on the time you spend on the bank is to walk up above the spot where the last angler started. So long as you arrive at the normal starting point at the appropriate distance behind the preceding angler, all is according to Hoyle. Occasionally you may be surprised by the results.

3. Do not waste everyone's time by waiting longer than it takes the preceding angler to get below the swing of your cast. If someone ahead of you in the rotation seems to be ignoring his time, ask politely if he intends to take his turn.

4. Once you have entered the rotation and are casting the maximum distance you intend, take one full step between each cast. If the preceding angler is moving more slowly than yourself, you have no choice but to adjust your speed to his. And do not wade out further than everybody else, even if you are convinced that the extra ten feet will let you reach the fish.

5. Stopping to retie or change a fly is permitted of course, but excessive changing of the fly during a rotation is self-defeating and irritating to others behind you. If you raise a fish you may take a step backward and recast once and/or change flies a few times without moving forward (subject to local variations). All this should not take any more than four or five minutes. If you have no success, you must move on.

6. If another angler hooks a fish you should reel in if you are close to him or downstream. Otherwise you can keep casting *but* don't move.

7. If you happen to be the lucky beggar with a fish on, you should deal with the salmon as firmly as possible to limit the amount of time the rotation is delayed. If possible, and the salmon may have a lot to say about this, try to prevent the fish from running downstream.

8. Once you land a fish you are expected to return to the start of the rotation. If you hook a fish and lose it without moving downstream you may resume casting, but if you have moved downstream, return to the start of the rotation. In other words, if the others have resumed fishing then you start over again. This is one of the rules that may be subject to local variation so, if possible, check this out with a regular before starting to fish.

9. While it should be obvious, upstream dry-fly fishing is out in a rotation situation.

10. Finally, if a situation arises that is not covered by the points above, follow the Golden Rule.

Even if you are fishing private water, and there are two or more people involved, the rotation system is sensible unless you come to another agreement.

Do these rules work? Absolutely! For those who have never encountered the situation it will seem virtually impossible that upwards of 50 anglers could fish a stretch of 150 yards. Many years ago, I fished Michael's Landing on the Main Southwest Miramichi most Saturdays during the open season. It was popular because the river was cut in two by a gravel bar which also curled in a hook shape across the top of the run. As a result, the water on the far side of the bar was normally too low for the migrating salmon's comfort. When a run was on, the stretch would be full of fish and you would find anglers on the near shore and working down the gravel bar. It was certainly crowded but a little courtesy and adherence to the rules mentioned above enabled more than twenty anglers to fish simultaneously. It was exciting because on some weekends fifty or more salmon would be taken from this spot.

Snagging salmon is reprehensible. If in your judgment a fast sinking line is required to properly present the fly, then *no* movement of the line by means of the rod or line hand is acceptable. The only action is provided by the current. If this seems overly restrictive when applied to very slow water or stillwaters, that's because it is. The ethical angler refuses to use methods that are subject to misinterpretation even if his intentions are honorable. All foul-hooked fish should be played very hard with no concern for loss and released immediately.

I'll get plenty of opposition on this next point, which has already been mentioned in Chapter 4 (for which I make no apologies). I believe it's unethical to fish for large salmon with very small dry flies; that includes anything smaller than size sixteen. The primary reason is that in many areas today, large salmon must be released. Very few of us are as capable of landing salmon as the late Lee Wulff, so our only recourse would be to apply light pressure and try to worry the fish to death. This is unconscionable when the intent is to release the salmon unharmed and capable of continuing the spawning run.

A secondary consideration is that a pricked salmon, which is the common result of using little hooks, is unlikely to rise again. This will spoil the chances of others for little gain. If the salmon are sulky and you get a big charge out of bringing a fish to the fly, then break off the hook.

You may encounter certain public rivers where some pools are fished by boat while others are frequented by wading anglers. The simple rule for this is to stay away from the boat pools unless you have reliable advice that a certain part of the pool has been "reserved" for waders. Occasionally a pool will be public on one side and private on the other with the private side being fished from boats. Courtesy is required by both parties and other than taking care not to cross lines when casting, little else is required.

Speaking of boats, those that use them in public water have a different code of ethics. It boils down to first come, first served. At Burpee's Bar in the St. John River, the boats are often launched at 2 a.m. in order to stake out the prime spots. In many ways, this is self-defeating but it's the custom and when in Rome, etc.

The required release of large salmon in Canada's Maritime Provinces places several additional burdens on the ethical angler. The first is to play the fish with as firm a hand as possible to reduce the dangers of excessive lactic acid accumulation. When this rule was first announced, some guides became overzealous and demanded that clients break off the fish after eight minutes. This was totally unnecessary but anglers should do their best to adhere to the minute-per-pound rule. It's a common but foolish practice of beginners to let a salmon run around to its heart's content.

Another concern is landing. As discussed in Chapter 9, tailing is a common way to land a salmon. But if the fish is to be released then it should not be lifted out of the water by the tail. Simply grasp the tail firmly and, holding the salmon horizontally in the water, release the hook. If you want to take pictures, after removing the hook, cradle the salmon with a hand under its belly and lift it gently just above the surface. It should go without saying that if the fish is to be killed the deed should be done as quickly as possible.

Parr are the future of the salmon fishery and should be treated like the little treasures they are. When you hook one, and it's likely you will, give them a bit of slack line first to see if they will come off of their own accord; if not, bring them in slowly, hold the hook firmly, and twist it out without taking the parr out of the water. Do your best to avoid touching the fish. Few things make me as angry as seeing an angler holding a hook in the air and vigorously shaking a parr.

One of the major reasons we fish for salmon is to visit the rivers where they swim. In most cases they are true, or semi, wilderness areas. Treat them with more respect than you do your own home. Leave no sign of your presence other than a little stone cradle where you have kept a grilse cool before returning to camp or a stick to measure the water level. Few anglers are as dedicated as my brother Jim who carries a garbage bag in the back of his vest to clean up the refuse left by the thoughtless. Finally, I want to mention a situation that poses considerable problems for a visitor to an area. What do you do if you witness an infraction of the law? Often the first reaction is to ignore the situation because of a fear of getting entangled in legal proceedings or worse. Even if you are prepared to act *do not interfere at the time*, unless of course it is apparent that the culprit is merely a novice acting out of ignorance. Fortunately, many regions have "report a poacher" programs that do not require anything more than a phone call. Take advantage of this opportunity to help protect the resource and your fishing.

Margaree River

Swinging Bridge — MSW Miramichi River

CHAPTER 11

WHERE TO GO (AND WHEN)

Recently, the famous British salmon fisherman Arthur Oglesby wrote, ''It might be expected that an experienced salmon angler like myself would be most frequently asked about the tactics needed to catch salmon. Surprisingly, the commonest question is: 'Where can I go and when?' It is also the hardest to answer satisfactorily.''

Salmon are creatures on the move — a fact which suggests both a general and specific answer to the ''when to go'' question. Generally, a river's salmon runs will come at the same times each year, given suitable water conditions. However, exactly where they will be found in the river depends on a host of variables. A vivid memory of my early days on the Miramichi was chasing the run. After a slow morning on the river we went on tour, visiting tackle shops and other pools, searching out reports of big catches. Then it was a matter of finding some public water where we could hope to intercept the fish.

As to where to go: In North America there are significant anadramous Atlantic salmon rivers in four Canadian provinces and the state of Maine. Because each has its own rules and opportunities, they will be dealt with separately. In general: 1) Always ask for references before booking with an outfitter, and do your best to find someone from your local area who has fished there. 2) If you intend to go exploring on your own, locate a tackle shop or other reliable source in the area beforehand, and then, the week before leaving, call and find out about water and fishing conditions. If the conditions are poor, consider changing destinations or postponing or cancelling the trip. Although there's more to fishing than fish, no one wants to feel beaten before starting. 3) Take the time to learn about the rivers you want to fish. There are excellent river guidebooks available for many areas and the cost, relative to your total outlay, is negligible. The following sections reference these sources and include ordering information.

Regardless of all advice, when you consider the conditions affecting the material success of a salmon-fishing trip, choosing a destination and a time remains a gamble.

NOVA SCOTIA

The wind gusted up the Margaree valley, dragging along rain squalls like the wash of perfume from the passing of a beautiful woman. A steady, heavy rain the night before had fed the river's appetite and swelled its belly. There was a pulsing, lively message in the wind. ''Fresh fish,'' it whistled. ''First pool,'' I hummed. Only a few others sang the same tune.

The upper section of the pool fished from the high right bank along which the water ran swift and deep. The curving shoreline produced a number of swirling eddies. Looking down the narrow path, which flirted often with the undercut edge, I quickly estimated my chances of surviving a cave-in before flicking out the first cast. Only hip waders were necessary to ward off the rain-soaked bushes or land a fish at the bottom of the pool, but I welcomed the warmth of chest-high neoprenes. During my first trip through the pool, a preceding angler hooked a fine salmon and I shot a roll of film of the fight and landing. During my second pass, the Alexandra, which had been sitting forlornly in my box for many years, drifted into an eddy and was accosted by a smaller fish that leaped, ran, and rolled for ten minutes before the hook pulled out.

Preparing for a fourth attempt I decided that the roiling muddy water called for a chartreuse Marabou Muddler and a sink-tip line. After several dozen casts I sense an unnatural tension and struck. Sixteen pounds of angry Atlantic came to the top and rolled heavily. His fate was release and I treated him roughly. We struggled for 200 feet downriver when the salar became insulted at my hard hand, sunk to the bottom and sulked. Years ago I would have irritated him to death. Now I pulled hard and broke the leader . . . there was a plane to catch.

Nova Scotia has a virtually unique tradition of public fishing waters. The Angling Act passed in the mid-20's claimed all lakes and rivers to the average high-water mark for the public and established the right to cross uncultivated private land to fish. It is a fine testimony to the conduct of most anglers, both non-resident and native, and to the goodwill of landowners that the law has gone unchallenged for more than sixty years.

An "open waters" policy has two major effects. First, it spreads the fishing pressure over a large area. Second, fragile fisheries require careful management to preserve their quality. To that end the major regulations affecting salmon angling are: all salmon exceeding 25.4 inches in length must be released, fly-fishing only, one unweighted fly tied on a single or double hook, and no weight added to the leader.

Nova Scotia treats visiting anglers well. For example, a one-season Atlantic salmon license is only a hundred dollars. As of this writing, guides are not required except for travel into the bush. However, it appears that this situation may change in the near future. The reason is increasing abuse of Nova Scotian hospitality. Too many non-resident salmon fishers are arriving in the province carrying everything they need to stay for a week or two, thus spending absolutely nothing in the local area. Revenue from tourism is important to the economy of Nova Scotia and these "visitors" are parasitic. They contribute nothing while enjoying a resource supported by the tax dollars of the residents. As a result, a requirement for non-residents to be accompanied by a licensed guide is expected soon.

Most Nova Scotian rivers are small. Consequently, the pools usually accommodate only a few anglers, and all practice the rotation system. There may be deviations, so ask questions. Ignorance of local customs will never be held against you on the bank, only in the water. Many rivers are easily wadable, but a couple, particularly the Medway, have unsuitable banks and so are fished almost exclusively from boats.

Recommendations for flies vary with the season: height, temperature, and color of water, the particular river, etc. Nonetheless, a few obligatory standards are Buck Bug and Bomber for both wet and dry fishing, Red and/or Green Butt, Butterfly, Blue Charm, and Marabou Muddler. Sizes 4, 6, and 8 will cover most normal and low-water conditions but a few Mickey Finns in 1/0 and 2/0 will come in handy should things turn high and dirty.

TABLE 3. SELECTED NOVA SCOTIA RIVERS

River	Average Catch CPRD	% Large Salmon	1991 Catch CPRD	Normal Season	# of Pools or Fishable Length	Comments
East Pictou Co.	254 .3	76	591 .4	1/09 31/10	15 Miles	Must have rain to bring fish, then fishes well.
Gold	366 .3	32	84 .1	10/05 31/08	20	Early river, fishes well with lots of water.
LaHave	1867 .3	27	395 .1	10/05 31/08	21	Consistent producer. Some boat-only pools.
Musquodobit	359 .1	33	261 .1	01/06 15/10	25 Miles	Beautiful river but low returns.
St. Mary's	1351 .2	26	1281 .2	01/06 15/10	18	Excellent early run of large fish.
Medway	693 .2	30	98 < .1	10/05 31/07	38	Fished from boats. Don't rotate.
Moser	197 .1	11	137 .2	01/06 15/10	14	Small river. Little interest to visitors.
Stewiacke	691 .1	36	213* .1	31/12 31/12	15	Pleasant late season angling. Friendly crowd.
Salmon Guysborough Co.	234 .2	35	367 .2	24/06 15/10	20 Miles	Wild country, worth exploring. Underfished.

Tusket	175 .3	32	122 .1	01/06 15/08	2 Miles	At the southern tip of N.S. Not for visitors.
Grand	481 .2	25	136 .1	01/06 15/10	13	Short river, fish move quickly on raise of water.
Margaree	1468 .2	52	2506 .2	01/06 31/10	31	Big fish river, best near end of season.
River Philip	200 .4	73	600 .4	01/09 31/10	10 Miles	Very dependent on water level.
North Victoria Co.	455 .3	71	507 .4	01/06 31/10	20	For hardy souls but the rewards are there.

NOTES: 1. Averages are over ten years where available.
2. 1991 was a very bad year for south shore rivers due to drought.
3. CPRD = Catch Per Rod Day
  *Stewiacke figures are for 1990. River closed 1991.

Management practices have resulted in substantial improvements in the salmon fisheries of Nova Scotia during the last several years. The purchase and removal of commercial nets, the halting of commercial fishing, the mandatory release of large salmon, and the examination of logging practices have all helped to revitalize many spawning runs. Unfortunately, on other rivers, the battle against acid rain has been lost or the remnants of once viable populations are struggling to survive. During the last decade Nova Scotia has lost some 13 rivers to acid rain, mostly in the southeastern part of the province. The tragedy is that these rivers are beyond all hope of restoration; the acid rain has leached all the buffering material from the surrounding watershed. Even the return of normal rain would now leave the water too acidic for successful salmon reproduction.

The accompanying table gives basic information for the principal Atlantic salmon rivers of Nova Scotia. The season is lengthy, middle of May until the end of October, but the best fishing is in the spring and fall. Most rivers have a "quality time" as shown in the table. The fall is popular with many non-residents because the hunting season draws many natives away from the rivers. According to the table, the number of rod days per fish averages around four. This is not considered outstanding fishing but compares favorably with other public salmon and steelhead waters.

Another year, another early morning on the Margaree. I headed out under clouds whose body odors reeked of rain. Back to the tidal pool? Yes, and it was all mine. On my second walk down the path, even closer to the edge than last year, there was a considerable splash within a foot of the bank near the end of the run. Seemed a strange place for a salmon to be holding; more likely it was moving up. Nonetheless, my casting became more deliberate as I reached the spot.

The black Marabou Muddler stopped cold at the end of the sweep and the line moved to the middle of the river. Without showing, the salmon sulked on the bottom, shaking its head. By the time they reached my hand, the resulting vibrations had been transformed to trembles of uncertainty. "Stick to your guns," I thought, applying maximum pressure, just as I had the year before.

This time the fish yielded and swam into the quiet water down-stream where leaps which seemed to thud in the air punctuated a fifteen-minute fight. Tailing the yard-long fish, removing the fly, and then watching it head out into deeper water after only a few minutes of gentle resuscitation reminded me of the words of the Earl Grey: ''After three years' study of Canada I am prepared to hold the field against the world — that great as are the resources, advantages and attractions of her sister Provinces, Nova Scotia need not be afraid to pit her charms against any of her sister Provinces, however fair they may be.''

TRIP INFORMATION

You reach Nova Scotia via air through the capital city of Halifax. Visitors from the Northeastern states can drive through New Brunswick or take the ferry from Bar Harbor, Maine, to Yarmouth. Access to most of the rivers is easy since they are along the coast and usually paralleled by roads.

Typical costs in Canadian dollars (the exchange rate fluctuates but at the time of writing was $1 US = $1.15 Can.) are:

Motels — $35–$50 per night for a double
Lodges — $600–$900 for two, for five days, all inclusive
Rental Cars — $200–$300 per week
Airlines — variable, of course, but the fall is a good time of the year for bargains

Unless your is an ultra-low budget adventure, I recommend a guide for your first day or two on the river. Try to get a recommendation from other anglers. Failing that, check in at a fly shop in the local area. Write to the province at the address given below and request a list of outfitters and a copy of the *Fishing Guide to Nova Scotia*. This useful map gives, among other things, the location and name of the pools on eight of the primary salmon rivers.

Other sources of information about the Margaree River, one of Nova Scotia's major destinations, are *Handbook for the Margaree* by James T. Grey, Jr., available at the Margaree Salmon Museum or order for $13 from the author at 107 Dolington Rd., Yardley, PA 19067; and *Fly Fishing The Margaree of Nova Scotia*, a Greycliff River Rap audio tape, available from Greycliff Publishing Co., Box 1273, Helena, MT 59624 for $13.95 plus $1.50 for p&h. *Salmon Rivers of Cape Breton*, authored by the same Mr. Grey, available as above for $9.00(sc) or $17.50(hc), covers other rivers on that rugged but beautiful island.

Should you decide to fish the rivers of Cape Breton, the Margaree Salmon Museum is certainly worth a visit. The history of salmon fishing on the river is represented by various displays, including rods and reels used by several famous visitors like Henry Van Dyke. Flies dressed by Lee Wulff, the Darbees, Megan Boyd, Poul Jorgansen, Colin Simpson, and a display of John Cosseboom's patterns can be studied. Along with a three-dimensional model of the river, the collection will hold your interest for several hours.

Write to the Nova Scotia Department of Tourism at PO Box 456, Halifax, N.S., Canada, B3J 2R5.

NEW BRUNSWICK

Writing in 1862, Robert Barnwell Roosevelt, a famous New Yorker, named the Nepisiguit as the best salmon river in New Brunswick. His views were shared by a number of other anglers like Charles Hallock and Richard Dashwood, who wandered the wilderness during the same period. At that time the Miramichi was being netted ruthlessly and the Restigouche had a poor reputation among flyfishers. While the Nepisiguit has rebounded recently after many years of neglect and the Restigouche still attracts a limited number of anglers (for a vastly different reason), the Miramichi is today's most popular destination.

New Brunswick has over a hundred streams and rivers where salmon swim but most of these have small runs of interest to local anglers only. The three great river systems are the Miramichi, Saint John, and Restigouche. The only other stream of interest to visitors is the Nepisiguit.

Open seasons are set for each river but there is bright salmon fishing available from June until November. The kelt season (more about this later) runs from April 15 to May 15. All non-residents must have a guide. Basic regulations concerning tackle and catch-and-release are the same as in Nova Scotia.

The Miramichi System

The greatest Atlantic salmon river in the world, depending on the yardstick, is New Brunswick's Miramichi River. Although comprehensive statistics are notoriously difficult to obtain, I found no recent claims (Russian rivers are unknown) of total runs exceeding the 150,000–180,000 salmon that most years enter the Miramichi between June and November. And of considerable interest to anglers, the system offers the most "public water" in the province.

Disregarding minor contributors, the Miramichi is really a system of seven rivers. Into the main stem, known as the Main Southwest Miramichi, flow the Cains, Bartholomew, Renous — joined by the Dungarvon, and Northwest Miramichi — joined by the Little Southwest Miramichi. The total length of the watershed is 769 miles, with 316 miles of "public water," most of this in the tributaries.

To avoid confusion, the phrase "public water" needs further explanation. In the last century, New Brunswick adopted the British legal theory of riparian rights. Such rights, where attached to an original land grant, conferred ownership of the river bottom to an adjacent property owner. In many areas the Crown retained or acquired these rights, thus giving it the authority to permit or restrict the public's access to these waters. For a non-resident, with a few exceptions, the public water is available providing you buy a license and hire a guide.

Early Spring Salmon

Like Inspector Fix following Phileas Fogg, the polar winds stalked me halfway around the globe. Having blown me out of Tasmania in December, they lay in wait among the spruces of New Brunswick until I arrived in April. Right on cue, as I lofted the first backcast from a perch atop an ice block, they swooped up and across the Little Southwest Miramichi to greet me. The forward cast promptly imitated a dying quail to center field.

TABLE 4 — SELECTED NEW BRUNSWICK RIVERS

River	Total Fishable Length (Miles)	Miles of Public Water	Average Catch	Average % Grilse	Average CPRD
Main S.W. Miramichi	153	17.6	15607	69	.54
Little S.W. Miramichi	104	24.	2982	80	.51
N.W. Miramichi	88	13.	4803	78	.46
Sevogle	69	48.	1386	79	.44
Renous	83	71.	1709	82	.42
Dungarvon	64	42.	565	78	.36
Cains	57	37.	941	59	.51
Bartibog	27	27.	229	55	.89
Tabusintac	26	16.	518	60	.49
Saint John	11	11.	2544	57	.26
Nashwaak	66	29.	1609	58	.15

TABLE 4 — SELECTED NEW BRUNSWICK RIVERS

1991 Catch	1991 % Grilse	1991 CPRD	Ave. Kelt Catch	1991 Kelt Catch	1991 Kelt CPRD	Comments
11724	69	.20	5430	6784	.76	Public water consists of many short sections but most are good water.
2279	65	.18	393	590	1.07	River has very consistent runs, probably due to its excellent spawning areas.
2362	74	.13	707	797	.72	Lower open stretches heavily fished by local anglers. Noted for large early grisle run.
456	74	.14				Small pools, very widely separated and requiring a 4x4 to reach in some cases.
993	78	.15				Small river with small pools. Best fished by walking sizable lengths of river bank.
775	62	.18				Small river but has many good and accessible pools.
1128	59	.21				Late-run river (Sep/Oct). Beautiful canoe float during normal water levels.
133	16	.15	111	105	.38	Small river but good return for effort.
238	65	.28	266	232	.47	Mostly fished by local anglers. Only one outfitter in the area.
1425	64	.10				Boat required in most areas. Not practical for visitors except with outfitter.
1403	65	.11				Usually has some fish throughout season. Late fall may be the best time.

TABLE 4 — SELECTED NEW BRUNSWICK RIVERS

River	Total Fishable Length (Miles)	Miles of Public Water	Average Catch	Average % Grilse	Average CPRD
Tobique	95	48.	1947	61	.23
Restigouche	232	8.	4078	51	.74
Upsalquitch	81	0.	1202	68	.64
Kedgwick	37	0.	593	58	.68
Nepisiguit	18	10.	1313	76	.30

NOTES: 1) Figures are for bright season in columns 3–8.
2) CPRD = Catch Per Rod Day
3) For information on all rivers phone 800 561-0123.

Wind aside, the prospects for tight lines were excellent. The end of April is usually right in the midst of the best action for spent salmon returning to the salt water. Referred to as kelts or black salmon, these fish willingly strike a fly when in the mood. But although they swim down all salmon rivers at some time, the only extensive spring fishery is on the Miramichi.

The number of salmon that over-winter seems to depend on the character of the river. The Miramichi system, with its gentle currents and large stillwaters, holds fish that under different conditions may head for the ocean right after spawning. Fortunately, on the Miramichi, a significant number of spawners of both sexes, perhaps as high as 80 percent, survive to form part of the next spring's kelt fall.

What about the impact of the world's most effective predator on the out-migrating stock? Evidence indicates that the catch-and-release rules in effect for multi-sea winter salmon provide adequate protection from anglers. In addition, many spring grilse are also returned. Studies of release mortality range from 5–15 percent,

TABLE 4 — SELECTED NEW BRUNSWICK RIVERS

1991 Catch	1991 % Grilse	1991 CPRD	Ave. Kelt Catch	1991 Kelt Catch	1991 Kelt CPRD	Comments
1954	63	.16				Traditionally fished from canoe. Headwater dam releases may affect fishing — pos. or neg.
1776	52	.22				Not practical for visitors except with outfitter.
1006	65	.28				Same as above.
566	43	.27				Same as above.
1733	69	.18				Outstanding success story of river enhancement and rejuvenation.

although that could certainly improve if all anglers would use barbless hooks and bring the salmon to hand quickly.

As a matter of historical interest, reasonable bag limits and concern for safe release were considered in the early years of the fishery. In a 1968 article, Charlie Wade recalled, ''. . . the angler could land ten salmon, including grilse, per day, and retain one,'' and ''The law requiring barbless hooks . . . was in effect for twenty-five years or more but this was finally changed, as practical barbless hooks were not on the market.''

Regardless of the kelts' reputation for hitting anything that moves, it wasn't until evening of the day mentioned earlier that I finally connected. In the stillness of a gently falling snow a grilse came to the hot orange steelhead fly as it swung through a run on the main river below Gray Rapids Lodge. The fight was certainly not that of a bright fish but compared favorably to a brown trout of similar size. Later captures of much larger specimens confirmed that opinion.

The early spring fishery dates from the turn of the century. While separate statistics have been kept only since 1960, the average kelt catch on the Miramichi comprises one quarter of the season's total. But you won't have any trouble finding lots of river to fish. And as can be seen in the accompanying table, the catch/rod day is much better than during the bright season.

And as can be seen in the accompanying table, the catch/rod day is much better than during the bright season.

Depending on their philosophy, anglers may be missing a good thing. The commercial fishing ban combined with the required release of all large salmon has resulted in a substantially increased kelt fall with the average size growing all the time. My set of values sees nothing wrong in casting a fly to a fish which has completed its spawning duties and is feeding aggressively. While it's true that the specimens which come to hand are not as pretty nor usually as strong runners as the fresh-run edition, I think of them as different fish. In the words of Clayton Stanley Stewart, native of the Miramichi Valley and former outfitter, ''I have moving pictures of hooked Salmon in both April and May jumping out of the water as many as fourteen times before being landed. There may be some lifeless ones, but it is the 'exception' rather than the 'rule.' ''

The salmon usually rest in slow pools and quiet eddies as they drop downriver to the sea. There are a number of ways to reach them. Based on limited experience, I prefer to cast from shore. Neoprenes make wading an acceptable proposition but there are drawbacks. Ice pans float silently downstream and the big ones can knock you into very cold water. Ground cover also enters the equation. Most anglers wear felt-soled boots, but when there is snow and mud underfoot, such footwear would be grounds for a sanity hearing. Normally, at the end of April the rivers have receded enough for shoreline casting, even if the ice, like enormous white riprap strewn carelessly along the banks, makes clambering around somewhat tricky. I'd suggest a pair of insulated knee-high rubber boots.

The other approach often favored by outfitters, is fishing from boats. Depending on the nature of the water, the angler casts a floating or sinking line or alternatively lets out a long sinking line and retrieves it with the reel. As casting forms part of my fishing pleasure, besides helping to keep me warm, I find the latter method unappealing. For safety reasons each angler must have his own guide when fishing from a boat.

Tackle should be suited to the conditions. Since all large salmon will be released, it is reasonable to use the heaviest equipment compatible with fishing comfort. While normally using an 8-weight, in the spring I go heavier; 9 and 10-weight outfits are recommended with an assortment of floating and sinking lines. Leaders testing ten or twelve pounds make sense because the salmon aren't leader-shy. Don't forget warm clothes and rain gear. April in New Brunswick is often spring only in the still-frozen dreams of the residents.

Streamer and bucktail patterns are popular, including everything from minnow-imitating patterns like the Black Ghost to the gaudiest of steelhead flies. Whatever else you bring, have some Mickey Finns in your book. One exciting development is the initial success of dry-fly addicts. While hardly explored to date, Bill Ensor, who toils to promote New Brunswick's fishing, has brought kelts to a big Bomber. If you encounter fish in low clear water, particularly in the tail of a pool, give it a try.

The Bright Season

A sticky purple stain accumulates in the creases of my fingers, courtesy of a handful of blueberries hastily stripped from a bush. Tongue and teeth sort ripe from green as I scan the river for a likely salmon lie. A half mile below where my brother Jim is tossing a fly, I get the feeling — not just the feeling of basting in sweat inside a neoprene skin that urges me to find cool water soon. No, something about the way the currents smoothly avoid the aggressive blocking tactics of a group of rocks beyond mid-stream triggers a salmon feeling.

I polaroid the bottom and decide where to begin covering the seventy-five yard stretch. Wading to the middle of the river and stripping out twenty feet of line, I direct the Cosseboom to caress the fabric of the watery cushion fronting the first promising rock. With the cast lengthened by three feet each time, the fly is soon sweeping the entire width of the likely water.

I enter that special space where the rhythm of the cast sands the tension-sharpened corners off the psyche, while simultaneously all my senses focus on the swimming fly. Ten steps downstream comes a sign. A faint swirl, a flash of silver side, an unnatural change in a shadow, I'm not sure. One step backward and another cast. Nothing! Step forward, cast again. Yes! The line stops. Just for a moment a heaviness and then a run. The reel's guts shriek with agony as line melts from the spool. The grilse is in the air, trying to touch bullet head to forked tail. Now he's down but the rod springs back and the line goes slack. Shoulders droop and head hangs while the reel gathers in the line he borrowed.

Releasing almost every fish I land, there's still an unfinished feeling when my hand doesn't get the chance to complete the act — a sense of personal failure no matter what the cause.

This was a trip I'd wanted to make for many years, a three-day canoe float of the upper reaches of the Main Southwest Miramichi River. The names of the rapids — Push and Be Damned, Big and Little Louey — are as colorful as the loggers who named them. But crossed signals found us at a halfway lodge the first evening, so the next day would be spent fishing around camp. After breakfast we worked a picturesque home pool shaded by towering pines. Sadly, the scent of their pungent sun-baked sweat wafted across apparently vacant water — hence my semi-successful stroll downriver.

Day three of our trip saw us headed for the takeout point, leap-frogging pools to fish, unsuccessfully. I became convinced that we were consistently going too deep into likely spots before anchoring, so eventually I asked to stop well above some fishy-looking water. Fortunately for me, we scored. The only landed salmon of the trip collected a Butterfly as it swirled past a rock at the head of a short slick.

The Miramichi's bright season opens at the end of the first week in June and continues on some branches until the end of October. Because of the main river's size, salmon enter it throughout the season, but in normal years there are major runs in late June/early July and September/October. Not all the tributaries are equally blessed; for example, the Cains sees very little action until the fall. Droughts play havoc with the timing of the larger runs and fall often produces the most consistent fishing.

Virtually every imaginable type of salmon water except for thunderous gorge pools can be found somewhere in the system.

At one time or another I've wetted a line in everything from brooks in the headwaters of the Northwest Miramichi to ponds surrounded by no-see-um infested bogs near the source of the Renous. Places like these are of little interest to the visiting angler because of the time required to reach them but they attract residents searching for solitude. Most of the popular water is in the lower stretches where the larger pools and longer runs hold more salmon and are less disturbed by angler activity.

For many years most of the Miramichi was closed by the end of September. The regulations left a substantial portion of the fall run unexploited. A few years ago, to the applause of most, the season was extended several weeks.

Heavily kyped males and the darker colors of both sexes mark these fall salmon as nearly ready to spawn. They don't fight quite as well as the summer runs but often make up for this defect by being more aggressive takers. Most anglers put away the dry-fly box during this season but those with more persistence still succeed. Even though the chances of getting rained out are somewhat greater, I would pick this season as your best chance to succeed.

The Miramichi Salmon Museum

Great clouds of smoke and sheets of flame engulfed the forest and the river hissed and steamed like a hot spring from the fall of burning embers. Such was the view from the present-day site of the Miramichi Salmon Museum of the conflagration that razed the Miramichi Valley in October, 1825. Since the museum's opening in 1983, visitors can read about the human and ecological tragedy of the great fire between viewing exhibits more commonly associated with the river's salmon-fishing history. Doaktown, New Brunswick, historically the center of the Miramichi system salmon angling, is the obvious location for a chronicler of the river's sporting heritage. Ideally situated on a hill overlooking a classic salmon run, one can watch from the deck of the River Room salmon fishers plying the waters each day of the open season.

First, immerse yourself in the ambience of the valley by viewing an audio/visual presentation providing background material on the river and its tributaries and the sport of salmon fishing. While all form part of the Miramichi system, the character and geology of rivers, such as the Little Southwest Miramichi and the Northwest Miramichi, are quite different. Bottoms vary from easy-to-wade gravel to more treacherous pocket water and the scenery changes from pastoral farmland to heavily forested woodlands.

Next spend some time with the exhibits of the work of many famous fly tiers. Flies tied by John Atherton, Preston Jennings, Ira Gruber, Bert Miner, Everett Price, Charles DeFeo, Jack Storey, Jack Sullivan, and Wallace Doak are highlights of the collection. The astute visitor will be able to trace the development of many of the distinctive Miramichi patterns. Modern artists who create presentation patterns or recreate the classic ties are represented by Ron Alcott and J. Martinez.

The museum receives international support. Collectors from all over North America loan or donate material like antique reel or rod collections to enhance the displays. Others who have fished the area for many years generously provided the photographs or other memorabilia so essential to the development of a collection.

Salmon fishing is a civilized field sport. Most anglers pause during the day to rest themselves and the pools. So when you visit the Grand Dame of salmon rivers, instead of wiling away the pause at the lodge, set aside several hours to enjoy the many fine exhibits of the Miramichi Salmon Museum.

The Restigouche System

The Restigouche system, which includes the Upsalquitch and Kedgewick, is celebrated for the size of its fish and the cost of getting near the water. It regularly delivers salmon in the forty-pound class, and two years ago an angler hooked and released a monster estimated at seventy-two pounds. If the measurement formula is accurate (and since this capture there has been plenty of argument) it was the second largest fly-caught salmon in recorded history.

Regrettably only a few fortunate anglers are ever likely to cast a fly over Restigouche waters. I was overwhelmed with jealousy when reading these incredible lines from Hallock's *The Salmon Fisher* (1890): ''Going back no farther than twenty-five years, it is easy to remember that mine was almost the only salmon rod upon the noble Restigouche throughout its majestic length of sixty miles of superlative salmon-fishing ground. . . . For two successive years I had it entirely to myself. . . .''

The Saint John River System

The soft evening sky touched with pink and orange tints stretched up above the earthen dam standing shoulder to shoulder with its concrete companion. A quarter mile downstream a fourteen-foot fiberglass canoe edged away from the bank into the current with a net peeling out from the stern like a gigantic tapeworm. Down went the bottom of the net, sinking under the influence of a leaded rope, settling to the bed of the river in ten feet of water. One hundred and twenty-five feet out, the black-painted buoy strained against its anchor and spoke to the night in a sibilant hiss. The net's floating upper strand, its far end fixed to a convenient rock on shore, was swiftly knotted to the buoy and the canoe put back to the beach. The boatman curled up on a soft patch of grassy soil, flipped the top off a bottle of beer, lit a cigarette, and quietly spoke to his fellow netsmen. They compared this year's run to the flood of fish ten summers ago.

Before each could have his say, a thrashing on the surface signalled the first capture of the evening. Down to the canoe and out into the river. A cigarette butt made a tiny red pinwheel as it traced out a parabolic path to extinction in the swirling ebony currents. Up came a section of the net with twelve pounds of aggrieved Atlantic salmon trapped by the nylon mesh pulled tight behind its gill covers. A priest ended the struggles and the first of a satisfactory evening's take lay quiet in the bottom of the boat. Before 3 A.M., one hundred and thirty pounds of leaping silver that would leap no more. Although less demanding than his ancestors' tradition of spearing under torchlight from the bow of a canoe, the good companionship and promise of a full freezer was creating a continuity with the social customs of the netman's past.

Five A.M., several years later on the same river, on the same shore, the sports and guides are gathering. The aluminum bass boats swing on their moorings just beyond the low-water mark. While canoes are traditional in salmon fishing, the squat interlopers combine additional stability with casting comfort. A skiff is launched to ferry the guides, and soon a confusion of outboard-motor exhausts shatters dawn's tranquility. By ones and twos, bows crunch into the gravel of the little beach and anglers follow their gear aboard. Reversing through the minor melee, the boats reach uncluttered water and push aside the river's currents on the way to the bar.

Chapel Bar, the stage where the netsman acted, remains unchanged, but the play and players are new — well not all new perhaps — some have simply changed costumes. The rewritten script is the result of an agreement between governments and the Kingsclear Band of the Malacite Indians whose land borders this section of the St. John River. A traditional food fishery was traded for the benefits of tourism.

"I vision this mighty river, the longest between the St. Lawrence and the Mississippi, and the most beautiful in North America before the dams at Beechwood and Mactaquac destroyed it for all time!" Thus wrote George Frederick Clarke about the St. John in his wonderful memoir of salmon fishing in New Brunswick, *Six Salmon Rivers and Another* (1960). Robbed of its reproductive capacity, the biologists decided it was most efficient to trap the returning salmon at Mactaquac, transport them to the hatchery for sorting and selection of brood stock, and then truck most of the rest above Beechwood dam to provide angling and some limited natural spawning in the Tobique River. There are still a few places to take salmon on the main river but Chapel Bar is the only one of interest to visitors. Regardless of the symbolism, it is always fascinating for an angler to witness a tank truck disgorging the spoils of a day's trapping at the dam into the holding tanks at the hatchery: sea run brown trout and steelhead, landlocked salmon from the headpond, gasperaux and shad all mixed with the king of the waters, the Atlantic salmon.

It's early and the gates of the great power houses are closed. A June morning's mist clings tenaciously to the black stones of the exposed portion of the bar. Billy says, "let's start here," as he cuts the motor and jerks the anchor line upward to free it from its "no hands" lock. The rope slides through two pulleys and the 30-pound lead cylinder slices through three feet of water and hits bottom quickly. The boat creeps downstream so fifteen extra feet of line are run out before the anchor grabs. We agree on a Green Machine and, after Turle-knotting the fly to the eight-pound tippet, I toss ten feet of line across the stream to begin the process of "fishing the drop." All the boats have found a hold. The engines are still. Peace and quiet has been restored, except for the occasional perturbation of the ether as a salmon falls through the surface following an inexplicable leap.

Later Billy took off his baseball cap, and reaching into the foam insert said, "well it's time for the killer." I agreed. One hazard of fishing under the gaze of a concrete icon is that the flow is controlled by people responsible for water control and power generation. "Too much water," grunted Billy. Regardless, the salmon were there. They teased the anchored anglers by leaping saucily, like supplicants eager to see the face of their master, as they stormed by on their way to gather at the cement feet of the giant.

Usually the river rises slowly during the first fishing session between 5 and 10 A.M. and has already begun to fall when the evening stint begins at 6 P.M. But when I fished here there was a heavy flow right through the day. The take was not impressive — particularly not when compared with the normal conditions of the week before. Averaging a very respectible .78 fish hooked per rod day, most between ten and sixteen pounds, Chapel Bar is one of the better Atlantic salmon fisheries in North America.

Normally, when fishing from a canoe, the angler is put ashore to fight a salmon. At Chapel Bar the fight takes place afloat because of the difficulty of getting the bass boats into the bank. This drawback can unreasonably lengthen the battle because the salmon will hang downstream, using the current to its advantage.

After a cast out to the right a movement pulled my eyes from the swimming fly. An osprey beat its wings ponderously to gain altitude with a squirming meal clasped in powerful talons, freshly scooped from the shallow water covering the bar downriver. Later Billy pointed out a family of eagles soaring on invisible currents high above the steep hillside to my left. Chapel Bar and its Atlantic salmon epitomize a frequently encountered dichotomy of our technological society. Upstream lies the hand of man at its most visible, a steel and concrete dam. Downstream stretches a pastoral valley with all its natural treasures on display. Fortunately our casts are downstream.

The Nashwaak River enters the Saint John across from the capital city of Fredericton. As there are no dams downstream from this point, the salmon stock remains a strain of wild fish. I spent many pleasant days wandering beside the Nashwaak's small pools where I learned a great deal about fishing little rivers. But the Nashwaak is of minor interest to the visiting angler because of limited runs spread out over a long season.

The Tobique is, sadly, a river I've never fished. Crossing it dozens of times on the way to Jim's lodge, it's an aperitif before the main course of the Miramichi eighty miles farther on. Although beholden to the tank trucks from Mactaquac (which often deliver upwards of 7000 salmon a season to the Tobique), its anglers are presently enjoying as much success as they did in the 1950's. Most importantly, it is a beautiful valley and Jim recommends the experience, particularly Little Bald Peak Lodge run by Al King.

The Nepisiguit

As mentioned at the beginning of this section, the Nepisiguit River near Bathurst was the favorite destination of the first enterprising anglers to visit New Brunswick. After a long period of decline it now yields a respectable catch each year. The large salmon average between 15 and 20 pounds, with a few going over 30.

There is only one outfitter on the river, Ken Grey, and it can be quite difficult to find a guide on your own. Fishing is reasonable all through the season, which runs from June 1 to October 7, but the biggest salmon arrive early. Ken tells me that the 15+ miles of open water don't see many resident anglers on weekdays.

In general, New Brunswick offers a wide variety of Atlantic salmon fishing opportunities. The visitor can hire a guide on a daily basis for around $75 a day (although this can prove difficult in some areas), buy a seven-day license for $50, arrange his own accommodations, and explore the public water. Or you can stay at a full-service lodge for between $800 and $2500 per week depending on

From the Boat — St. John River

Godbout River

the amount and quality of private water available and the level of
luxury you need to make your stay comfortable. As for equipment,
the chapter on tackle covers the requirements.

For further information on New Brunswick, write to: Department of Economic Development and Tourism, P.O. Box 6000, Room
516, Centennial Building, Fredericton, N.B., Canada E3B 5H1, Attention: Bill Ensor.

QUEBEC

One June, while returning from the Godbout river on Quebec's
north shore, I reflected on what I'd spent for a week's fishing. It
was four hundred dollars Canadian, including gas, food, lodging,
license and rod fees — about average for a trout trip. Quebec is
an attractive proposition, with the bonus of being the only place
in Canada (other than a few Labrador rivers) where you can keep
a large salmon.

Quebec counts at least 106 salmon rivers. However, the
Ministère du Loisir, de la Chasse et de la Pêche (MLCP) provides
statistics for only sixty-two. This is because many rivers have runs
too small to be worth managing or are presently sanctuaries. For
convenience, I group the rivers into five geographical areas, the
North Shore as far as Havre-Staint-Pierre, the Gaspe Peninsula,
the remainder of the North Shore, Ungava, and Anticosti Island.
Only the first two are covered in detail because the other three areas
are strictly high-buck propositions involving full-service outfitters
and/or substantial transportation costs.

Historically, salmon fishing in the province was virtually the
prerogative of wealthy English Canadians and Americans. In 1976
a socialist provincial government took over many leases and created
local management authorities. The conflicting objectives of increasing public access and enhancing the resource spawned a complicated system of open water, reservations, and draws. Cutting
through this Gordian knot of regulation takes great patience and
undeniably favors the resident angler.

Many rivers combine two or more of the following: private club,
outfitter lease, advanced reservation zones, night-before-draw sec-

TABLE 5. SELECTED QUEBEC RIVERS

River	Zone 1	Zone 2	Zone 3	Zone 4	Average Catch ___ CPRD	Average Weight ___ % Grilse
Gaspe Region	Note 1	Note 1	Note 1	Note 1	Note 2	Note 3
Matane	U ___ 5	P	U ___ 67		719 ___ .14	8.1 ___ 32
Sainte-Anne	P	14 ___ 41	4 ___ 13	2 ___ 10	423 ___ .30	12.1 ___ 18
Madeleine	P	U ___ 85			294 ___ .29	9 ___ 35
Dartmouth	U ___ 17	6 ___ 6	U ___ 9		284 ___ .22	10.6 ___ 16
York	SEE REMARKS				702 ___ .37	12.5 ___ 9
Saint Jean	6 ___ 15	6 ___ 24			500 ___ .34	9.2 ___ 15
Grande-Rivere	U ___ 30	3 ___ 8	U ___ 8	4 ___ 5	262 ___ .25	3.1

TABLE 5. SELECTED QUEBEC RIVERS

1991 Catch / 1991 CPRD	How Fished	Cost	Season	Comments
	Note 4	Note 5	Note 6	
854 / .17	W	Z1&3 30.00	25 JUN / 30 SEP	Recommended. Fishers are learning to rotate the pools. Info: 418 562-3700
599 / .37	C & W	Z2 — 45.00 / Z3 — 335.00 / Z4 — 65.00	25 JUN / 15 SEP	Z3 has 4 rods with outfitter. Z2 has 8 preseason, 6 48hr; Z3 has 4 preseason; Z4 has 2 preseason. Info: 418 890-6527
322 / .23	C & W	Z2 — None	15 JUN / 31 AUG	Upper River (Z2) recently opened. Rugged area! Canoe is required during early season or high water. Info: Steve Whiting 418 393-2605
417 / .22	W	Z1 — 30.00 / Z2 — 50.00 / Z3 — 30.00	1 JUN / 31 AUG	Z2 has 4 preseason & 2 48hr reservations. The 4 pre-season are a draw. Z3 best after 1 Jul. Info: 418 368-2324
684 / .21	W	25.00 to 65.00	11 JUN / 31 AUG	Z1, 5, 7, 11 — unlimited rods (18 pools); Z4 & 9-10 pre-season, 8 48hr (21 pools); Z2, 3, 6, 8 — total 12 48hr (9 pools). Info: 418 368-2324
646 / .43	C & W	Z1 — 45.00 / Z2 — 450.00	11 JUN / 31 AUG	Z1 all preseason. Z2 outfitter. Info: 418 890-6527
251 / .20	C & W	Z1 — 35.00 / Z2&4 — 50.00 / Z3 — 30.00	11 JUN / 31 AUG	Canoe required in Z1. Z2 has 4 48hr. Z3&4 require 4wd for access. Info: 418 385-3940

TABLE 5. SELECTED QUEBEC RIVERS (Continued)

River	Zone 1	Zone 2	Zone 3	Zone 4	Average Catch / CPRD	Average Weight / % Grilse
Bonaventure (Note 7)	U / 8	A + B / 14 / 55	U / 11	U / 15	1259 / .34	9 / 22
Matapedia	U / 4	10 / 26	U / 36		1620 / .22	12.3 / 26
Petite Cascapedia	P	8 / 35			115 / .28	9.2 / 30
Cascapedia	SEE REMARKS			6 / 6	1005 / .34	17.6 / 5
North Shore						
St. Jean (Saguenay)	P	6 / 6	4 / 4		217 / .27	9.2 / 37
Ste. Marguerite	U / 12	16 / 16	U / 14	16 / 22	571 / .17	9.5 / 25
Godbout	U	12 / 12	P	U / 40	879 / .40	5.1 / 51

TABLE 5. SELECTED QUEBEC RIVERS

1991 Catch / 1991 CPRD	How Fished	Cost	Season	Comments
1098 .27	C & W	Z1, 3, 4 35.00 Z2 — 55.00	11 JUN 31 AUG	Z2A has 5 preseason & 5 48hr. reservations. Z2B has 4 48hr. Canoe required in June or during high water. Info: 418 534-1818
1461 .22	C & W	Z1 — 35.00 Z2 — 345.00 Z3 — 35.00	11 JUN 31 AUG	Z1 has considerable private water. Only 4 of the 39 pools are open. Z2 — outfitter. Info: 418 890-6527
195 .34	W	Z1 — 215.00 Z2 — 35.00	11 JUN 31 AUG	Z1 is private but an outfitter owns several pools & leases several more. Z2 has 4 pre-season & 4 48hr. Info: 418 392-5001
895 .24	C & W	Z4 — 50.00	1 JUN 31 AUG	1 rod/day on Z1, 2, 3 with preseason bookings. Little chance for non-residents. Z4 has 6 48 hr. Rod may be shared. Info: 418 392-5079
277 .34	W	Z2 — 9.00 Z3 — 20.00	18 JUN 21 AUG	Z2&3 are private property on which the owner charges for use of the river. Info: Z2 — 418 272-2073; Z3 — 418 272-2955
520 .18	C & W	Z1&3 — 27.00 Z2&4 — 42.00	11 JUN 30 AUG	Large salmon in June. Z2&4 have 14 preseason & 2 48hr. accommodations at reason-able rates. Info: 418 236-4604
514 .23	W	Z1 — 15.00 Z2 — 28.00 Z3 — 25.00	15 JUL 15 SEP	Only Z4 worthwhile. Some Z4 pools require a long walk. Z1 is tidewater. Z3 — 12 beats. Info: 418 568-7565

TABLE 5. SELECTED QUEBEC RIVERS (Continued)

River	Zone 1	Zone 2	Zone 3	Zone 4	Average Catch CPRD	Average Weight % Grilse
Trinity	15	U			708	5.3
		52			.30	2
Moisie		SEE REMARKS			1486	16.5
					.30	2
St. Jean	U	P	26		645	9
			N/A		.51	10

NOTES: 1) Zones are the way the local river authority has grouped the pools for the purposes of allocating fishermen. P = Private water. Top figure is number of rods permitted (U = Unlimited) and the bottom figure is the number of pools in that zone.
2) Averages span varying time periods depending on data availability. CRPD is Catch Per Rod-Day.
3) Average weight in pounds is the top figure. Percent grisle is the bottom figure.
4) W stands for wading. C means canoe required or recommended.
5) Cost is daily rod fee in addition to basic salmon permit. Figures are a guide and are subject to change.
6) For Gaspe Rivers — normal open season dates, for north shore rivers — dates are first and last capture of salmon in 1986.
7) Zones 2A has 15 pools. Zone 2B has 40 pools which can only be reached by canoe.

tors, unlimited access pay-by-the-day stretches, and unlimited free-access areas. Table 5 highlights these divisions, but further explanation is required. Advance reservations, normally good for three days, are made on a first-come, first-served basis, usually by phone. The phone lines open at a specified hour on a day between January and March depending on the river. Typically you have thirty days to make your deposit or your sections go back into the pot for a redraw. On some rivers you have a choice of sections or group of

TABLE 5. SELECTED QUEBEC RIVERS

1991 Catch / 1991 CPRD	How Fished	Cost	Season	Comments
473 / .26	W	Z1 — 37.00 / Z2 — 27.00	3 JUN / 8 SEP	Z1 has 8 preseason & 6 48hr Z2 has excellent fishing. Info: 418 939-2242
2290 / .27	C & W		Varies with zone	Public water not practical for non-resident. Three outfitters, 900.00-2000.00 for 3 days, all inclusive. Info: 418-962-3737
574 / .42	C & W	Z3 — 300.00 to 450.00	15 JUN / 31 JUL	Z1 is tidewater. Z3 — outfitter with 2 camps, leases over 40 miles of river. Info: 418 949-2547 (Day) or 949-2843 (Evening)

pools, again on the first-come, first-served principle. But on others you may have a pool or beat rotation schedule imposed, either by a prearranged schedule or an early-morning draw.

Many rivers also feature forty-eight hour advance reservations and/or a nightly draw. Only a few rods are usually involved so it doesn't pay to count on this to get fishing. However, as these sectors may include quality waters or serve as a chance to get some privacy, it doesn't hurt to join in every evening if you're already flogging the proletarian pools. In addition, most river managers market unsold reservations in accordance with a locally established published policy. My advice is to ignore the pre-season reservation system (although the word from a few of my friends is that it is getting easier) unless of course you plan to book a trip with an outfitter.

The basic salmon license for non-residents costs $43.50 (remember there are additional daily rod fees just about everywhere) and is issued with seven blue seals for the tagging of salmon (depending on the location, you may be entitled to an additional three tags). This represents your season limit. The daily limit is complicated. If you land or release a large salmon, that's it. If you release a grilse you may continue fishing until you hook another fish. But now you are finished for the day whether or not you release it. There are limited exceptions to these rules.

In my opinion, these rules discourage the releasing of fish and may unreasonably diminish the quality of the experience. It would appear that either an unsubstantiated concern with release mortality or a desire to allow unsuccessful anglers additional opportunities is behind this regulation.

Quebec does not require non-resident anglers to employ a guide when fishing most areas. However, certain advanced reservation sectors do (mostly those that include canoe floats), and guides are naturally a part of outfitter packages. The daily rod fee for the zone in question tells the story.

Now to a situation which may appear to be a larger source of problems than it is. The language of Quebec is French. Experienced foreign travelers will be accustomed to dealing with language difficulties in day-to-day matters of ordering food, etc.; however, you may, for example, have problems in making advance registrations or in understanding the complexities of the rules and regulations of the various draws.

A summary of the general regulations is available in English from any of the addresses listed below. You can get information on individual rivers from the local management authorities at the telephone numbers in the table. I have verified that most can provide information in English but there are exceptions. Also, the MLCP office responsible for a particular region will send you addresses and other useful information if you prefer to write. In any event, the majority of Quebecois(es) are friendly people and will try to help surmount any language difficulties. One unpleasant residual of the "colonial" period is that resident anglers (and therefore a number of visitors who follow their lead) have been slow to accept the concept of an orderly and amicable rotation of rods through the pool. However, there has been a marked improvement in fishing manners on certain rivers during the last few years.

Quebec's North Shore (Côte Norde) is rugged country where the villages hug the coastline and the blackflies dwarf their southern cousins. Even today, almost half the region remains accessible only by aircraft or ferry. The first designated salmon river is the Du Gouffre, some 248 miles from Montreal, while the Romaine marks the end of the road 446 miles farther on. In between are twenty-two salmon rivers of which eight merit inclusion in the table. Upon reflection, only the Ste. Marguerite, Godbout, and Trinity have sufficient unlimited access water to interest the budget-conscious visitor. All three rivers are located in areas with plenty of reasonably priced accommodations. The Laval, not included in the table because the average catch is very small, is worth a try if you are in the area when the fish are there because the average size of the fish is large — around 20 pounds.

Beyond Havre Saint Pierre there are a number of excellent rivers, some with unlimited free access. But, as noted earlier, these can only be reached by boat (or aircraft) and aren't the kind you visit on speculation. Conveniently, there are vehicle ferries from a number of North Shore ports to Matane. If the fishing is poor you can always cross to the Gaspe where conditions may be better.

Salmon rivers compete with spectacular scenery in the Gaspe. The closest important river is the Matane, which André Boucher, former Director of Public Relations of the MLCP, calls a salmon fishing school. Each of its classic pools fishes differently, requiring adjustment in casting angle to achieve the optimum swing of the fly. On the opposite side of the peninsula the Matapedia joins the Restigouche river just before it enters the Bay of Chaleur. That's about a two-hour drive across or a twenty-hour drive around. Actually, as the most accessible (open water) sectors of both rivers are well upstream, they are much closer than two hours.

My recommendations for planning a trip to the Gaspe are as follows:

1) a minimum of two weeks is essential to avoid the dreaded lament, "the conditions were all wrong."

2) as the rivers are nicely grouped, stay in Matane (2 hrs. to the Matapedia), Gaspe (Dartmouth, York, St. Jean, with the Madeleine and Grande-Riviere within 1½ hrs.), or Bonaventure (Bonaventure, Petite Cascapedia, Cascapedia). There are plenty of campsites in these areas in addition to motels. Call the information numbers in the table for recommendations.

3) ignore the reservation lotto until you arrive and plan to fish the unlimited rod sectors.

4) pay for only one or two days at a time to stay flexible.

5) canoe rentals are reasonable but avoid unless you are experienced.

6) regarding flies, if you tie your own, bring a selection of Rats, Cossebooms and Green Highlanders in sizes 2/0 to 8 and a collection of Bombers, Buck Bugs and Wulffs but be prepared to buy a small supply of whatever's "hot!"

7) order a copy of *Gruenefeld's Atlantic Salmon River Log — Gaspe Region* from George Gruenefeld, PO Box 5352, Station B, Montreal, Quebec H3B 4B5 ($22.95 Canadian including shipping). This valuable book offers a wealth of information about each river and will be a welcome companion while planning and taking your trip.

Now to the table. You will find information on all rivers with a significant run of fish and which are accessible by car. Each is divided into one or more (up to four) zones depending on the way it is managed. The top figure in each box is the number of rods permitted in that zone each day and the lower one is the number of pools which those rods may fish.

Take the Bonaventure River for example. The local river management has divided the pools into four zones. An unlimited number of rods are permitted to fish the eight pools in Zone 1, the eleven in Zone 3 and the fifteen in Zone 4. You may arrive at any time, without reservations, and by paying the daily rod fee, fish one of these three zones. Zone 2 has been subdivided into two sub-zones A and B. To fish the fifteen pools in Zone 2A you must make advance reservations. Five rods, for two-day periods, are made available for reservation, by phone, starting at 9 A.M. on the second Saturday of March. This means that if you are lucky enough to get through, you could reserve two rods for say, June 17 and 18, or some other available dates. There is a maximum of two rods for a two-day period allowed per phone call. Now, there are an additional five rods in this same zone that are made available each day, for one day, forty-eight hours before the date in question. In other words, you could reserve one rod (maximum per call) for June 19, by phoning on June 17 (phone lines open at 8 A.M.).

Next comes Zone 2B with forty pools for four rods, for which only forty-eight hour reservations are accepted. Zones 2 and 3 have a daily rod fee of $55. As is true with most rivers, you can purchase a membership card (usually around $25) that reduces your daily rod fee by up to $10. It's also worth noting that a rod may be shared on the Bonaventure. This means that two people (both must be registered) may fish on one daily pass but only one may fish at a time. Once you make a tentative decision as to which river(s) you plan to fish it is *absolutely essential* that you get further information. Rivers have varying dates for advance reservations, rules governing shared rods, and pool accessibility.

Columns 5 and 6 present a five-year average (where sufficient data was available) of the total catch, angler effort, weight and percent of grilse in that order. As a comparison, column 7 lists the 1991 catch and effort statistics. The prices provided in column 8 change frequently and so are only a guide. As is evident for the zones that are controlled by outfitters, the price includes food, lodging, and guide. Some establishments offer an American Plan at a reduced rate.

For the Gaspe, column 9 gives the dates the season opens and closes, but for the North Shore, the dates represent the earliest and latest date that a salmon was caught in 1986. Note that the various zones on a river may each have their best times so you *do* need additional advice. For example, there is fishing on the Godbout from June 1 to September 15, but I would not recommend the river until after July 15 because the upper section doesn't open until sufficient fish have cleared the falls. The lower section has very limited fishing and my experiences with its organization were negative. On the other hand, the September dry-fly fishing may be spectacular.

The comments are based on personal experience or conversations with knowledgeable anglers and the telephone numbers were valid as of March 1992. The saying that ''proper planning prevents poor performance'' is certainly applicable and I strongly recommend a call ahead to the river(s) of your choice for an up-to-date report on the fishing conditions.

Quebec has much to offer the angler in search of Salmo salar. Arrive with the attitude that goodwill and patience can overcome any minor irritation, and the reality of leaping silver without a second mortgage should be your reward.

INFORMATION

For all areas including Anticosti and Ungava:

MLCP
Communications Office
150, Boul. Saint-Cyrille Est
Quebec, Quebec G1R 4Y1
Telephone 418 643-3127

For information on Gaspe

MLCP
92, 2nd Rue Ouest
Rimouski, Quebec G5L 8B3
Telephone 418 722-3830

For information on the North Shore

MLCP
818, Avenue Laure
Sept-Iles, Quebec G4R 1Y8
Telephone 418 968-1401

NEWFOUNDLAND AND LABRADOR

I've never visited "The Rock" and so rely on conversations for much of the following information. One authoritative source was Len Rich, formerly promoter of Newfoundland for the Department of Tourism and now the regional coordinator for the Atlantic Salmon Federation. Len also wrote *Newfoundland Salmon Flies . . . And How to Tie Them* (no date).

Although the province boasts nearly two hundred salmon streams, many have small, short duration runs of interest only to local anglers. On the island itself the Humber River system is considered the jewel of the fishery, although badly chipped. Salmon begin arriving the first week in June and remain available with fresh additions until the closing in mid-September. The largest specimens, which used to exceed thirty pounds, show up near the end of the season. The lower Humber is a boat fishery and visitors should hire an outfitter from the Gander area. The Codroy is another reasonable choice and still yields the odd 20–30-pound fish.

The region made famous by Lee Wulff, the River of Ponds and Portland Creek, has been decimated. Easy access and severe interception netting have reduced the runs to a trickle. In fact the whole western shore of Newfoundland has suffered badly. Recent regulation changes eliminating netting in this area mean the fishery has excellent future prospects.

Realistically, Laborador rivers are only available through outfitters. The Eagle is the foremost fishery. Should you book into these areas and the salmon fail to show, there are opportunities for various species of char and trout to ease the pain. The Pinware and Porto Rivers on the southern coast of Labrador are also producers of large salmon, and outfitters are available.

Today, Newfoundland requires all non-resident salmon anglers to have a guide — two anglers may share a guide. The average cost is $100 per day. All waters are public, which in this case is a mixed blessing. While you have access to the island's rivers, the failure of local anglers to accept the rotation system significantly diminishes the value of this freedom. Contacts tell me that unless you connect with an outfitter who can get you to remote waters, or arrive later in the season after many local anglers have taken their limit, be careful. Tackle and flies recommended follow the advice given in chapters 6 and 8.

For further information contact: Department of Development and Tourism, P.O. Box 8700, St. Johns, Nfld., Canada A1B 4J6, Phone 1-800-563-6353.

TABLE 6. SELECTED NEWFOUNDLAND AND LABRADOR RIVERS

River	Average Catch CPRD	91 Catch CPRD	Comments
Humber	2721 .37	1508 .26	Best river in Nfld. for large salmon. Boats req. in lower section.
Gander	1908 .24	1180 .20	4 large ponds. Need guide and boat to move around.
Exploits	1608 .24	1045 .18	Longest river in Nfld. Vast variety of fishing situations, wadable.
Conne	1377 .30	108 .16	Small river. Gets good run in early June.
River of Ponds	1373 .39	1328 .46	Can reach good water with outfitter. Late Aug. = Dry fly.
Grand Codroy	1353 .26	1469 .30	Big river in lower part which sees local pressure. Need guide with boat.
Grey	529 .90	514 .71	Best catch per rod day on island. Remote, 1 outfitter available.
Gambo Brook	760 .41	802 .55	Short. Hard to figure. Difficult wading. Good guide a must.
Main River (Sops Arm)	558 .53	537 .29	Extremely pretty. Crystal water. 4 outfitters available.
Indian Brook (Indian River)	555 .36	413 .26	Not so pretty (clearcutting). Easy access. Provincial park.
Garnish	548 .30	491 .24	Small river, early run, easy wading.
Grandy Brook	874 .45	419 .35	Mid July best (low pressure). Good dry fly water.
Labrador Rivers			
Pinware	927 .37	974 .43	Outfitter only.
Sandhill	441 1.17	215 .31	Outfitter only.
Eagle	1362 .84	851 .60	Outfitter only.

Note: CPRD = Catch Per Rod Day

MAINE

The history of the Atlantic salmon in the New England states is as well known as it is sad. The remnants of this great fishery struggle for survival in a few rivers in Maine. While there have been several attempts to restore runs to historic levels in a number of rivers, the only semi-success story is the Penobscot. This isn't meant to belittle the efforts of those who have worked so hard to accomplish the resurrection, just a comment on how far is left to go to reach numbers like the estimated 35,000–70,000 that ran the river in pre-colonial times.

Because only the Penobscot yields sufficient fish to be of real interest, I haven't provided a table. During the past six years this river has had an average catch of 620 salmon. The best year was 1990 with a catch of slightly over 1000 and in 1991 it was 422. I could not locate angler-effort statistics. Other rivers that occasionally yield a salmon (always less than 60 and usually less than 10) are the St. Croix, Dennys, E. Machias, Machias, Narraguagus (the best of this group), Union, Ducktrap, Sheepscot, Androscoggin, Saco, and Kennebec.

Most of the salmon from the Penobscot are taken in the Bangor area; a pool map is available from the Maine Council of the Atlantic Salmon Federation. The largest salmon caught in recent years was a 22-pound 7-ounce fish, landed in May of 1988. Records suggest that you should show up at the same time as the main run of salmon enters the Penobscot, between May and the first of July. Fishing can also be good, depending on water levels, in the fall.

Regulations differ from river to river but on the Penobscot in 1991 the season limit was five fish, of which one could be over 25 inches. Catch-and-release is taking hold and during the better years almost two thirds of the captures go free. For a complete summary of the regulations, write to the address given at the end of this section.

The popular flies include most of those discussed in Chapter 8, in particular, Black Bear with various colored butts, Cosseboom, Rusty Rat, Butterfly, Bomber, and White Wulff. There are a number of locally developed favorites including the Wringer and the Ver-

Margaree Salmon Museum

Spring on Little Southwest Mirimachi River (Milton McKay photo)

Jim Marriner before catch and release (Gerry Williamson photo)

Wallace Doak's Tying Bench, Miramichi Salmon Museum

Doubleheader — St. John River

Dartmouth River, Quebec (John Huff photo)

Matapedia River, Quebec (John Huff photo)

St. Anne River, Quebec

Western Newfoundland River (Len Rich photo)

Penobscot River, Maine (Jane Cleaves photo)

Normal river — Dungarvon River

Mike Crosby's Restigouche Monster (Photo courtesy Mike Crosby)

dict. Sizes vary from 5/0 to 8 depending on water height and temperature.

For a copy of the regulations, write to: Maine Atlantic Sea Run Salmon Commission, P.O. Box 1298, Bangor, Maine 04402-1298. For pool maps and other information, write to: Maine Council Atlantic Salmon Federation, P.O. Box 398, Brewer, Maine 04412.

WRAP-UP

You will have noticed that I have given few recommendations concerning guides or outfitters. The reason is that I have virtually no experience with them, having spent my time on public waters or with my brother, who became my licensed guide after I moved away from New Brunswick. I do know that you will be well taken care of by Guy Smith, who presently operates Gray Rapids Lodge.

One final thought: be prepared to be blanked. Some people wait several years for their first salmon, although others crack the champagne right away. Atlantic salmon fishing has a long history and an ambiance all its own. Enjoy the atmosphere, the stories, the rivers, and the rhythm of the cast, and you'll be happy to treat an encounter with Salmo salar as a bonus.

CHAPTER 12

ODDS AND ENDS

THE BEST TIME OF DAY

Dean Sage, who fished the Restigouche for many seasons, wrote in *Salmon and Trout* (1902), ''Therefore the angler who, undiscouraged, hopeful and careful, has his fly the most hours on the water, is sure to rise the most fish.'' That rather obvious advice aside, he felt 8 A.M. was early enough to begin and preferred the hours between 4 P.M. and twilight. My experience is that while the period between 11 A.M. and 2 P.M. has been prosperous, I've taken salmon from dawn to dark. All things being equal, with a limited number of days astream each year, I fish as much as I can.

Of course, things are rarely equal. If you are on your own or with a group in an area where a guide is required, some negotiation will likely be necessary. Many guides, not surprisingly, don't want to spend all day on the river because their fee is based on the specific number of hours worked. If an eight-hour day is the arrangement, then I'd choose 9 A.M. to 1 P.M. and 4 P.M. to 8 P.M. Should an outfitter be your choice, then the hours will have been determined by the owner. In New Brunswick this is usually 8 A.M. to noon and then 4 P.M. to 9 P.M. (in the summer). Check the hours before you sign up; I wouldn't stay anywhere that offered less than eight hours of fishing per day, and not the standard workday of 8 A.M. to 4 P.M.

WEATHER AND THE STATE OF THE WATER

All serious discussions of these two matters are pointless. You fish when you can or, depending on how badly you want to catch salmon, whenever you will enjoy it. I absolutely refrain during thunderstorms because I don't fancy standing around with a lightning rod in my hand.

No sage whose words I've devoured, or angler to whom I've spoken, disagrees with the position that salmon take best when the water is falling after a rise. Most believe the salmon move during the high water and are more interested in a fly after settling into lies in a new (to them) pool. Nonetheless, I've hooked fish at all states of water except a raging flood, and even then I'll nibble at the edges of the flooded banks with hopeful casts.

FIRST OR LAST?

Does it make any difference if you are the first or thirty-first person to fish through a pool? To this day I would rather be first than last, especially through small pools, but there is plenty of contradictory evidence. For example, some years ago my son James, brother Jim, friend Jerry Williamson, and I visited the North Branch of the Renous. James and Jerry went downstream, Jim and I up. We learned after meeting again several hours later that James, a complete novice, had landed and released a 16-pound salmon and retained a grilse while fishing behind Jerry, an expert angler. And the pool where this happened is small.

STALE SALMON

For several years I fished the Nashwaak River several times every week during the season. One summer there was a large salmon that stayed in a deep, slack eddy for almost a month during a low-water period. It seemed to be swimming continuously and would execute a head-and-tail rise every ten minutes or so. Every trick in the book was tried by many anglers but this fish was having none of it. I felt a strange sense of sadness for that salmon. It seemed to me a trapped creature, continually tracing out the limits of its cage, unable to continue the important journey. After a few attempts, I left it alone.

I've encountered other salmon acting similarly and never had any success with them. Nor have I heard of other anglers doing much better. Don't waste hours working over fish like this unless there is absolutely no other hope.

JUMPERS AND ROLLERS

Without a shred of proof, I believe jumping salmon are either moving or preparing to move. To my knowledge there is no scientific explanation for this activity, so feel free to speculate — everyone else does. In any event, although the occasional running salmon has taken my fly, fish on the move are poor odds and this may explain the belief that jumpers are rarely caught. Despite that, all salmon anglers are overjoyed to see a jumper, for beyond the sheer exuberance of the performance, it signals that the fish are active.

Rollers, excepting the stale inhabitant discussed above, are a source of unalloyed celebration. They are surface-oriented salmon which you can confidently expect to seduce. Don't leave a roller unless forced to by rotation requirements.

GUIDES

This is a touchy and difficult subject. To no one's surprise, there are good and bad ones. As a general rule, the average quality of guides is better in places where you don't have to hire one. Don't expect great service if you simply arrive in an area that requires a guide by regulation and hire one on a day-by-day basis. In these circumstances you may also be expected to transport the guide. It bears repeating that you should get a recommendation from a friend or trusted acquaintance if at all possible. One hint — good guides don't pick up a rod unless you ask them to demonstrate something.

Staying with an outfitter is a different story. You have a right to expect competence. The guide should be familiar with the water and know the lies at most heights of water. He will know the productive patterns and concentrate on watching the water for rises. If boats are involved and you don't have confidence in the way the guide is handling the craft, ask for someone else. Often the guides will be rotated among the anglers every day and the question of tipping arises. A normal tip is 15 percent and it should be given at the end of the day if changing guides, or at the end of the trip if not.

It seems ridiculous to have to say this, because the people who need to hear it don't read books, but guides are not servants. Most will offer to carry some of your gear if you have to walk to or between pools, but don't expect it. If you have a health problem, mention it to the outfitter when booking and to the guide before starting out. This should avoid any misunderstandings.

In my opinion, alcohol has absolutely no place on the river. It is even illegal in many places to transport or consume it away from your lodgings. Suit yourself after the fishing day is done.

FINAL THOUGHTS

Atlantic salmon fishing draws anglers for a variety of reasons. Among them are beautiful habitat, big hard-fighting fish, and the challenging mystique of a species that has no business being interested in our flies in the first place. Although past treatment of Atlantic salmon by man is an ugly story, the future is hopeful. An end to much of the netting, the purchase of quotas from the high-seas fishery, catch-and-release regulations, an environmentally aware public — all point toward a resurgence of the populations.

Just as I was completing this book, salmon fishers received some wonderful news. The Canadian government announced a five-year moratorium and voluntary buy-out of commercial salmon licenses in Newfoundland and Labrador. Because these fisheries intercept salmon on their way to Eastern Canadian and Maine rivers, we can expect significant improvements. Much of the credit for this program goes to the Atlantic Salmon Federation and associate organizations which have worked hard for many years to convince the government of its necessity.

BIBLIOGRAPHY

Aflalo, F.G., *A Fisherman's Summer in Canada*, London, Witherby, 1911.

Anderson, Gary, *Atlantic Salmon and The Fly Fisherman*, Montreal, Salar Publishing, 1985.

Anderson, Gary, *Atlantic Salmon, Fact and Fantasy*, Montreal, Salar, 1990.

Ashley-Cooper, John, *The Great Salmon Rivers of Scotland*, London, H.F. & G. Witherby, 1987.

Ashley-Cooper, John, *A Line On Salmon*, London, H.F. & G. Witherby, 1983.

Ashley-Cooper, John, *A Salmon Fisher's Odyssey*, London, H.F. & G. Witherby, 1982.

Atherton, John, *The Fly and the Fish*, Rockville Center, NY, Freshet Press, 1951.

Aubert, Gilles; Bellemare, Andre-A; Bilodeauu, Gerard, *Saumon Atlantique*, Montreal, Sentier Chasse-Peche, 1988.

Balfour-Kinnear, G.P.R., *Catching Salmn and Sea Trout*, London, Thomas Nelson & Sons, 1958.

Balfour-Kinnear, G.P.R., *Flying Salmon*, London, A & C Black, 1947.

Balfour-Kinnear, G.P.R., *More About Trout and Salmon*, London, Thomas Nelson & Sons, 1963.

Barr, David ed., *Salmon Fishing in Scotland*, London, Queen Anne Press, 1981.

Bashline, L. James, *Atlantic Salmon Fishing*, Harrisburg, PA, Stackpole, 1987.

Bates, Joseph D., Jr., *The Art of The Atlantic Salmon Fly*, Boston, David R. Godine Publisher Inc., 1987.

Bates, Joseph D. Jr., *Atlantic Salmon Flies and Fishing*, Harrisburg, PA, Stackpole, 1970.

Bates, Joseph D. ed., *The Atlantic Salmon Treasury*, Montreal, The Atlantic Salmon Association, 1975.

Bridges, Antony, *Modern Salmon Fishing*, London, Adam & Charles Black, 1939.

Buckland, James, and Oglesby, Arthur, *A Guide to Salmon Flies*, Ramsbury, The Crowood Press, 1990.

Calderwood, W.L., *Salmon!*, London, Edward Arnold & Co., 1938.

Chalmers, Captain Ian, *Salmon Fishing in Little Rivers*, London, Adam & Charles Black, 1938.

Chance, Jack (Ed.), *Fly Fishing for Salmon*, London, A. & C. Black, 1973.

Cholmondeley-Pennel, H., *Fishing* (Salmon & Trout), Boston & London, Little, Brown and Co. and Longmans, Green and Co., 1885.

Clarke, George Frederick, *Six Salmon Rivers and Another*, Fredericton, Brunswick Press, 1960.

Clarke, George Frederick, *Song of the Reel*, Fredericton, Brunswick Press, 1963.

Crossley, Anthony, *The Floating Line For Salmon And Sea-Trout*, London, Methuen Publishers, 1939.

Crowe, Philip Kingsland, *Out of the Mainstream*, New York, Charles Scribner's Sons, 1970.

Currie, W.B., *Days and Nights of Game Fishing*, London, George Allen & Unwin, 1984.

Dashwood, Richard Lewes, *Chiploquorgan; or Life By The Campfire in Dominion Of Canada And Newfoundland*, Dublin, Robert T. White, 1871.

Davy, Sir Humphrey, *Salmonia*, New York, Freshet Press, 1970, reprint of the 1828 edition.

Dawson, Major Kenneth, *Casts from a Salmon Reel*, London, Herbert Jenkins, ND.

Dawson, Major Kenneth, *Salmon and Trout in Moorland Streams*, London, Herbert Jenkins, 1928.

Dawson, Major Kenneth, *Successful Fishing for Salmon and Sea Trout*, London, Herbert Jenkins, 1951.

Day, Frank Parker, *The Autobiography of a Fisherman*, New York, Doubleday, Page & Co., 1927.

Dube, Jean-Paul, *Salmon Talk*, Clinton, NJ, Amwell Press, 1983.

Dunfield, R.W., *The Atlantic Salmon in the History of North America*, Ottawa, Department of Fisheries and Oceans, 1985.

Dunham, Judith, *The Atlantic Salmon Fly*, San Francisco, Chronicle Books, 1991.

Eaton, Roy, (ed.), *Trout and Salmon Fishing*, Newton Abbot, David & Charles, 1981.

Falkus, Hugh, *Salmon Fishing*, London, H.F. & G. Witherby, 1984.

Frodin, Mikael, *Classic Salmon Flies*, New York, Bonanza, 1991.

Fulsher, Keith & Krom, Charles, *Hair-wing Atlantic Salmon Flies*, North Conway, NH, Fly Tyer, 1981.

Gawthorn, G.E.J., *Never Bow to the River*, Upton-upon-Severn, Johnathans, ND.

Graesser, Neil, *Advanced Salmon Fishing*, Woodbridge, NJ, The Boydell Press, 1987.

Graesser, Neil, *Finer Points of Fly Fishing for Salmon*, Woodbridge, NJ, The Boydell Press, 1989.

Graesser, Neil, *Fly Fishing for Salmon*, Woodbridge, NJ, The Boydell Press, 1982.

Gray, L.R.N., *Torridge Fishery*, London, Nicholas Kaye, 1957.

Green, Philip, *New Angles on Salmon Fishing*, London, George Allen & Unwin, 1984.

Grey, James T., Jr., *Handbook For The Margaree*, Yardley, PA, published by the author, 1976.

Grey, James T., *Salmon Rivers of Cape Breton Island*, Yardley, PA, published by the author, 1984.

Hallock, Charles, *The Fishing Tourist*, New York, Harper & Brothers, 1873.

Hallock, Charles, *The Salmon Fisherman*, New York, Harris, 1890.

Hartman, Robert, *About Fishing*, London, Arthur Barker, 1935.

Hewitt, Edward R., *A Trout and Salmon Fisherman for Seventy-Five Years*, New York, Charles Scribner's Sons, 1948.

Hill, Frederick, *Salmon Fishing, The Greased Line on Dee, Don and Earn*, London, Chapman & Hall, 1948.

Hodgson, W. Earl, *Salmon Fishing*, London, A. & C. Black, 1927.

Hughes-Parry, J., *A Salmon Fisherman's Notebook*, London, Eyre & Spottiswoode, 1955.

Hunter, W.A. ed., *Fisherman's Pie*, London, A & C Black, 1926.

Hutton, John E., *Trout and Salmon Fishing*, Boston, Little, Brown, and Co., 1949.

Jones, J.W., *The Salmon*, London, Collins, 1959.

Jorgensen, Poul, *Salmon Flies*, Harrisburg, PA, Stackpole, 1978.

Kelson, Geo. M., *The Salmon Fly*, Goshem, The Angler's and

Shooter's Press, 1979 (facsimile edition).

Knowles, Derek, *Salmon on a Dry Fly*, London, H.F. & G. Witherby, 1987.

LaBranche, George M.L., *The Salmon and the Dry Fly*, New York, Charles Scribner's Sons, 1924.

Lanman, Charles, *Adventures in the Wilds of the United States and British American Provinces*, Vols. 1 & 2, Philadelphia, John W. Moore, 1856.

Little, Crawford, *The Great Salmon Beats*, London, David & Charles, 1989.

Little, Crawford, *Success with Salmon*, London, David & Charles, 1988.

MacKenzie-Philips, Peter, *Successful Modern Salmon Flies*, London, Blandford Press, 1989.

Mansfield, Kenneth, ed., *Salmon and Sea Trout*, London, Barrie & Jenkins, 1973.

Maxwell, Mike, *The Art and Science of Speyfishing with a Double-Handed Flyrod*, Vancouver, Gold-N-West Flyfishers, 1990.

McClane, A.J., *The Complete McClane*, New York, E.P. Dutton, 1988.

McLaren, Charles, *Fishing for Salmon*, Edinburgh, John Donald Publishers, 1977.

Menzies, W.J.M., *Salmon Fishing*, London, Philip Allan, 1935.

Mills, Derek and Graesser, Neil, *The Salmon Rivers of Scotland*, London, Cassell, 1981.

Moore, Phil H., *The Castle Buck*, New York, Longmans, Green & Company, 1945.

Netboy, Anthony, *Atlantic Salmon — A Vanishing Species?*, Boston, Houghton Mifflin, 1968.

Nobbs, Percy E., *Salmon Tactics*, London, Philip Allen, ND.

O'Gorman, *The Practice Of Angling*, Dublin, William Curry, 1855.

Oglesby, Arthur, *Fly Fishing for Salmon and Sea Trout*, Ramsbury, The Crowood Press, 1986.

Oglesby, Arthur, *Reeling In*, Ramsbury, The Crowood Press, 1988.

Oglesby, Arthur, *Salmon*, London, Queen Anne Press, 1986.

Pattillo, T.R., *Moose-Hunting Salmon-Fishing*, London, Sampson Low, Marston & Company, 1902.

Perry, Bliss, *Pools and Ripples*, Boston, Little, Brown, and Company, 1927.

Pryce-Tannatt, T.E., *How to Dress Salmon Flies*, London, Adam and Charles Black, 1977 edition.

Rennie, John, *"I Have Been Fishing"*, London, Seeley Service, 1949.

Richards, Coombe, *Salmon*, London, Herbert Jenkins, 1956.

Righyni, R.V., *Advanced Salmon Fishing*, London, Macdonald & Jane's, 1973.

Russell, Jack, *Jill and I and the Salmon*, Boston, Little, Brown and Co., 1950.

Sage, Dean et al., *Salmon and Trout*, New York, The Macmillan Co., 1902.

Scott, Jock, *The Art of Salmon Fishing*, London, H.F. & G. Witherby, 1933.

Scott, Jock, *At the Sign of the Split Cane*, London, H.F. & G. Witherby, 1934.

Scott, Jock, *Fine and Far Off*, London, Seeley Service, 1952.

Scott, Jock, *Greased Line Fishing For Salmon*, Philadelphia, J.P. Lippincott, circa 1936.

Shaw, Fred G., *The Science Of Dry Fly Fishing and Salmon Fly Fishing*, London, John Murray, 1907.

Sheringham, Hugh & Moore, John C., (eds.), *The Book Of The Fly-Rod*, London, Eyre & Spottiswoode, 1936.

Silver, Arthur P., *Farm-Cottage, Camp and Canoe in Maritime Canada*, London, George Routledge & Sons, ND.

Simpson, Major R.C., *Floating the Line to a Salmon*, London, William Earl & Co., 1947.

Smedley, Harold Hinsdill, *Fly Patterns and Their Origins*, Muskegon, Westshore Publications, 1950.

Smith, Captain A.P.R., *Salmon Secrets Shared*, London, Adam & Charles Black, 1950.

Stewart, Dick and Allen, Farrow, *Flies for Atlantic Salmon*, Intervale, Northland Press, 1991.

Sutherland, Douglas, *The Salmon Book*, London, Collins, 1982.

Taverner, Eric, *Fly-Tying For Salmon*, London, Seeley Service, 1947.

Taverner, Eric et al., *Salmon Fishing*, London, Seeley Service, 1935.

Ulrich, Heinz, *How the Experts Catch Trophy Fish*, Cranbury, NJ, A.S. Barnes, 1969.

Vieth, Frederick Harris D., *Recollections of the Crimean Campaign*, Montreal, John Lovell and Son, 1907.

Waddington, Richard, *Catching Salmon*, London, David & Charles, 1978.

Waddington, Richard, *Fly Fishing for Salmon — A Modern Technique*, London, Faber and Faber, 1950.

Waddington, Richard, *Salmon Fishing*, New York, Charles Scribner's Sons, 1948.

Waddington, Richard, *Waddington on Salmon Fishing*, London, The Crowood Press, 1991.

Weeks, Edward, *The Miramichi Fish and Game Club*, Fredericton, The Brunswick Press, 1984.

Wells, Henry P., *The American Salmon Fisherman*, New York, Harper & Brothers, 1886.

Wertheim, Maurice, *Salmon On The Dry Fly*, New York, Author, 1948.

Wetherell, W.D., *Upland Stream*, New York, Little, Brown & Co., 1991.

Wood, Ian, *My Way with Salmon*, London, George Allen & Unwin, 1957.

Woods, Shirley E., *Angling for Atlantic Salmon*, The Angler's & Shooter's Press, Goshen, NY, 1976.

Wright, Leonard M. Jr., *Fly-Fishing Heresies*, New Jersey, Stoeger Publishing, 1978.

Wulff, Lee, *The Atlantic Salmon*, New York, A.S. Barnes, 1958.

Wulff, Lee, *Leaping Silver*, New York, George W. Stewart, 1940.

Wulff, Lee, *Lee Wulff on Flies*, Harrisburg, PA, Stackpole, 1980.

Index

This is a limited index. Certain rivers and flies occur so often in the text that it is pointless to list all the pages where they occur. Instead, only major discussion references are indexed. Also, a number of rivers in the text are mentioned only in a historical context, these are indicated by (h). Books in the text are in bold, as is the page on which the dressing for a fly occurs.